Brazilian Jiu-Jitsu

A Comprehensive Guide to BJJ Grappling Basics for Beginners and a Comparison with Japanese Jujitsu

Table of Contents

Introduction

Are you interested in learning about Brazilian Jiu-Jitsu? Also referred to as the gentle art, BJJ (Brazilian Jiu-Jitsu) became prominent during the early '90s when Royce Gracie, a Jiu-Jitsu expert, won three times (first, second, and fourth rankings, respectively) in the Ultimate Fighting Championships.

Gracie's opponents were much larger and underwent extensive training in other styles and techniques like wrestling, karate, Muay Thai, and boxing, but he was still able to defeat them. His success was why Jiu-Jitsu became a popular MMA style, where the main focus is on ground fighting.

BJJ is a martial art technique that gives even weaker and smaller participants the chance to defend themselves successfully against stronger and larger attackers. It focuses on ground fighting, grappling, and applying joint locks and chokeholds to defeat opponents. It also involves punches, throws, and kicks.

The key is leverage, enabling even someone small to learn and master the technique.

The good news is that anyone can learn and master Brazilian Jiu-Jitsu. All it takes is to access the right material and training that tackles every important detail and how to do it. The material in this book is written with the reader in mind, focusing more on detailing the actions and techniques you can do to perform this martial art.

The most important aspect of Jiu-Jitsu is grappling, and you can efficiently master it with this book as your guide. What's great about this reading material is that it is written so you can easily understand concepts, techniques, forms, and any other important aspects of BJJ quickly. It makes use of simple terms for you to grasp easily.

After reading, expect to know most, if not all, of what you need to know about BJJ and begin your journey towards becoming a Master. Putting the knowledge you gained here into practice, you will enjoy the rewarding benefits of practicing BJJ, including better balance and coordination, self-discipline, confidence, and mental focus.

I highly advise pairing up this material with relevant Brazilian Jiu-Jitsu videos so you can gain a more active visual input. In this way, it will be easier to follow the techniques and instructions in this book.

Chapter 1: What Is Brazilian Jiu-Jitsu?

Brazilian Jiu-Jitsu, otherwise referred to as BJJ, is a form of martial arts with techniques that focus more on grappling. This grappling-based martial art also emphasizes the use of leverage and techniques that can force opponents to submit through chokes and joint locks. It is widely recognized as a highly effective method of unarmed combat, which continues to rise in popularity since it is constantly represented in global combat sports organizations like the UFC.

A Brief History of BJJ

The roots of Brazilian Jiu-Jitsu can be traced to Japanese Kodokan Judo, a martial art adapted originally from Jigoro Kano's Japanese Jujutsu. Since Judo was classified as a martial art, it consisted of the throwing strategies from Jujutsu together with the groundwork. The ground focus was limited, making it relative to BJJ's revolution.

In 1904, one of the top experts of Judo groundwork, Mitsuyo Maeda, traveled from Japan to different places around the world to teach Judo. His teachings mainly emphasized ground fighting techniques. Maeda reached Brazil in 1914, where he also started teaching and tried to build a Japanese community.

Carlos Gracie, one of Maeda's students in Brazil, studied under him for about five years. Gracie passed the techniques he learned from Maeda onto his four brothers, and in 1925 they opened the first Jiu-Jitsu academy in Brazil.

Gracie's brother, Helio, had poor health and small stature. As a smaller person, he was encouraged to pay more attention to using the techniques Maeda taught. He started working on and adapting even the most basic techniques and concepts of Judo by integrating leverage. His adaptation increased the possibility of even smaller opponents to fight – and beating larger ones.

He also started to experiment with Judo's basic techniques to modify and improve them. It led to the evolution and development of Gracie Jiu-Jitsu, more popularly recognized as Brazilian Jiu-Jitsu, a more effective yet gentle version of the art.

Also, at the time when Judo evolved, there were a few changes in the rules, reducing the emphasis on groundwork and focusing more on throws. This also limited the use of legal joint locks. During this time, BJJ started to emerge as a different sport from Judo. In BJJ, participants are permitted every takedown from Judo.

Aside from that, Helio Gracie put a lot of emphasis on full-contact fighting when practicing BJJ, including strikes and increasing the sport's practicality as a form of self-defense. These rules caused BJJ to keep on evolving as a distinctive and unique fighting system in Brazil.

This further led to no-holds-barred competitions where BJJ participants competed with other martial art disciplines in fights that had no rules. Due to these competitions, the effectiveness of BJJ as a unique fighting system became widely recognized.

In 1972, Carley Gracie left for the US and started teaching BJJ there, and Rorion Gracie followed him in 1978. As Brazilian Jiu-Jitsu became more and more popular in the US, Rorion Gracie, among others, founded the Ultimate Fighting Championship.

During the early stages of UFC, Royce Gracie showed how powerful BJJ was by beating martial artists who were prominent in many other disciplines. The effectiveness and power of BJJ were also demonstrated to a wider audience in the first UFC event made available in pay-per-view.

Significant Highlights in BJJ History

- **1925** - Academia Gracie de Jiu-Jitsu, the first school for practicing the sport, was opened by Master Carlos Gracie.

- **The 1990s** - Brazilian Jiu-Jitsu started gaining recognition in the US. It was also during the '90s that Royce Gracie scored a win against a strong opponent who practiced another form of martial arts. He earned that title during the Ultimate Fighting Championship (UFC).

- **1994** - the founding of IBJJF (International Brazilian Jiu-Jitsu Federation). The goal of this organization is to regulate and govern the sport's competitions.

Core Concepts and Aspects of Brazilian Jiu-Jitsu

Brazilian Jiu-Jitsu's core and fundamental concepts involve bringing any fight to the ground. It is all about the use of pins when attacking opponents and performing attacks through a submission.

Every time you are at the bottom, you should set a goal of creating space by shrimping and bridging and creating distance through wedges and frames. This is also possible by using leverage to flip your opponent over, providing an opportunity to be in a more dominant position.

Note: the core concepts and fundamentals of Jiu-Jitsu have to be applied in every concept, technique, and position of this sport. While this sport continues to adopt new methods and techniques, the fundamentals of the sport that serve as their underlying basics remain unchanged.

Therefore, you must constantly remind yourself that the primary focus of BJJ is to beat opponents by bringing them to the ground, as this form of martial art is all about ground grappling. BJJ requires you to take your opponent to the ground as it is the only way to take away his power and the chaos caused by fighting while in a standing position.

Bottom and top positions are considered the core of BJJ since these are the only available options while opponents are both on the ground. Learning to change to more dominant positions and escape dominant positions to beat opponents and survive is necessary.

While practicing BJJ, you will encounter new and modern techniques; some may be shelved. The core concepts, however, will stay, proving that they are indeed fundamental. Several techniques applied in BJJ will demonstrate how these fundamentals operate.

For instance, the scissor sweep demonstrates how important grips, leverage, off-balancing, and creating space are when sweeping or knocking the opponent over.

Understanding the 4-Step System

When learning and understanding Brazilian Jiu-Jitsu's basic rules and concepts, familiarizing yourself with the 4-step system vocalized by John Danaher will help. This 4-step system involves taking opponents to the ground, passing the legs, working your way through the pins' hierarchy, then attacking using a submission technique.

Implementing this system requires a total of three positions – standing, ground bottom, and ground top. The first step involves taking the opponent to the ground, and the goal is to stay away from the natural volatility of fighting while in a standing position.

The advantage of bringing the fight down to ground level is that it eliminates the power your opponent may create using his arms and legs. You can then pass the legs, which is crucial in getting rid of the dangers imposed by your opponent. Use your legs to kick, sweeping you over to get into a bottom-ground position.

After passing the legs, your goal is to achieve and maintain a dominant position. Your focus is on knee-on-belly, back mount, mount, and side control positions, as they are considered the core. Since they are the top core positions, it helps you obtain that ability to keep your opponent under control.

Moreover, it enables you to strike, set up, and implement a submission technique with only minimal risk. It is like being in a chess match where you need to be one move ahead in order to gain an advantage over your opponent.

Hand-to-Hand Combat Ranges

Hand-to-hand combat, which is also crucial in Brazilian Jiu-Jitsu, has three major ranges or categories.

Standing Position and Free Movement

Most matches or fights start in the standing position. If the fighter throws kicks and punches, it is called the striking range. Many striking arts, like boxing and kickboxing, usually spend much of their time in this range. Most grappling arts also begin matches and fights from a standing position, though it often quickly goes to the clinch, the second range.

Clinch

The clinch range is when the fighters grab and hold each other in a standing position. Since both fighters are still standing, it is also referred to as standing grappling. Other martial arts which specialize in clinch or standing grappling are Greco-Roman wrestling, sambo, Muay Thai kickboxing, and Judo.

The clinch's main goal is to stop or soften punches, set up throws and takedowns, establish strikes from the clinch, and block takedowns until one fighter breaks away. The ultimate goal will always depend on the situation and the current position of the combatant.

Ground Fighting

The third range is ground fighting, which occurs when one of the two fighters no longer stands. While several forms of martial arts perceive being on the ground as a failure, Brazilian Jiu-Jitsu will train you to bring your fight there deliberately. Ground fighting is what you should specialize in when practicing Brazilian Jiu-Jitsu. It's also essential to focus on training in other grappling arts, such as wrestling, Judo, and sambo, which also require you to spend a considerable chunk of your time fighting on the ground.

Why Does BJJ Focus on Ground Fighting and Grappling?

Fights and matches that last longer than usual will most likely move through the clinch, and it is from this range that fighters take the match to the ground. In most cases, being on the ground results from an intentional takedown, schoolyard tackle, or losing your balance, such as while tripping or getting rocked due to a strong punch.

One crucial fact to remember is that the Gracies earned an excellent reputation by sticking to the premise of the participant preventing themselves from being knocked out while standing. Their goal was to control their opponent once they were already on the ground. They were trained to use a few crude takedowns, leading to ground fighting, that put them in a position to take full advantage of their opponents' inexperience and unfamiliarity with this specific range.

When practicing BJJ, remember that the sport does not have a lot of resets to standing, making it different from other forms of martial art. Additionally, you will not win outright through pinning, unlike in Judo or wrestling.

With that in mind, BJJ fighters have to stay biased toward ground fighting as it is the specific area where most matches lead and remain on the ground if you continue to let the match flow naturally.

Positional Dominance Hierarchy

Another of the most fundamental concepts and theories to know about Brazilian Jiu-Jitsu is positional hierarchy or dominance. This concept involves specific positions that produce better or worse results, so it is crucial to be aware of them and know what to do whenever you encounter them.

Knowing positional dominance or hierarchy will give you a clear understanding of what occurs within the fight on the ground, helping you to protect yourself and possibly helping you win the fight. If you are on the dominant or top side, the traditional hierarchy will be:

- Rear mount
- Mount
- Knee-on-belly
- Side control
- Turtle
- Half, open, then closed guard

If you get into the bad or bottom side of the above-mentioned positions, expect this traditional hierarchy to flip, too, meaning the worst out of the mentioned positions will be on top, followed by the lesser ones working down to the different poses.

To beat your opponent successfully, you must maintain a dominant position as much as possible. You will know you're in a dominant position if you can easily maintain it instead of escaping it. A dominant position is also one that provides you with leverage and mechanical advantage. It keeps you safe from submissions and strikes, giving you plenty of opportunities to end the match through submissions or strikes against your opponent.

During a BJJ match or fight, you score points as you progress and move through various dominant positions while on the ground. Here's a view of BJJ's scoring system based on dominant positions.

- Rear mount = 4 points
- Passing the guard = 3 points
- Mount = 4 points
- Takedown from standing = 2 points
- Knee-on-belly = 2 points
- Sweep from guard = 2 points

Position before Submission

Brazilian Jiu-Jitsu also operates on its traditional mantra, which is "position before submission." This means that a secure and safe positional hierarchy is more significant than submission.

For instance, it would not be wise to make your opponent submit if you are still in a bad position or within his guard. It is also not advisable to fall or jump into arm bars that are vulnerable to failing, putting you at risk of being underneath him.

As you gain more experience and skills in the sport, you can adjust your mantra because improvements in your skills will make you more confident and secure in your potential escapes and defenses.

In other words, despite having failed submission attempts, the skills you have learned from training and experience help you recover confidently and try another more effective position. However, beginners must stick to the mantra, as it requires focus on position before submission – which is the basis of BJJ.

Benefits of Learning BJJ

Now that you know about BJJ's core concepts and fundamentals, it is time to learn more about the benefits you can attain from learning this ancient martial art. In this section, you will learn more about the benefits of learning Brazilian Jiu-Jitsu and what it can do for you.

A Form of Self-Defense

By practicing Brazilian Jiu-Jitsu, you will learn moves that will prove useful whenever you are in a situation where you need to protect yourself, particularly in a physical confrontation. As a proven self-defense system, BJJ will train you to defend yourself whenever you are attacked, and you will know exactly how to take your attacker to the ground, control him, and prevent him from hurting you.

Better Physical Fitness

Undeniably, Brazilian Jiu-Jitsu is a great form of exercise. Each sparring round, otherwise known as a roll, lasts for around 5 minutes but includes various low and high-intensity movements with only minimal rest. BJJ is indeed a fantastic workout requiring anaerobic and aerobic endurance. Spending half an hour of hard rolling helps you burn around 500 calories.

Good for Your Mental Health

Another incredible benefit of Brazilian Jiu-Jitsu is that it can improve your mental health. It is even an effective stress reliever, which can boost your mood. Every time you roll on your mat to practice Jiu-Jitsu, you get the chance to disconnect yourself from the world and the surrounding worries.

Brazilian Jiu-Jitsu even helps you live in the present, which is beneficial for building your self-esteem and creating a positive self-image. Since it is suitable for mental health, it can help you avoid depression and anxiety.

Builds Discipline

The mental and physical challenges you will likely encounter when practicing BJJ will build and foster discipline. For instance, the requirement to attend classes every week without fail already develops discipline. You also have to be disciplined when dealing with losses during sparring, which is essential in attaining growth.

Improves Problem-Solving Skills and Creative Thinking

Your problem-solving and creative thinking skills will be put to the test when you practice Brazilian Jiu-Jitsu, which is why many also refer to this sport as a game of human chess. You must constantly adapt to various body types, techniques, and styles in this martial art.

Expect your brain to be trained to think creatively and calmly, even when under stress and pressure. It also trains your brain to overcome and handle complex problems. Your ability to adapt and think fast will also be honed as you will encounter different challenges each time you practice the sport.

Going out of your comfort zone is possible if you constantly practice BJJ. This sport will challenge you to grow and learn something new constantly. You will be trained to conquer your fears and pursue things that you thought were previously impossible. BJJ martial art is, therefore, valuable for your personal growth.

Chapter 2: Tips That Everybody Doing BJJ Should Know

As you will probably have learned by now, Brazilian Jiu-Jitsu is about martial art based on the ground, which incorporates different chokes and joint locks to beat an opponent. Anyone who has experience with Judo or wrestling will immediately realize that Jiu-Jitsu requires a unique and different challenge.

Before putting your opponent into submission, it is important to take your opponent to the mat. Once on the ground, you will use your Judo skills and take advantage of various takedown techniques and throws. While on your feet, BJJ requires spending most of your time doing throws, wrestling techniques, and trips.

Standing is also vital in BJJ, but it focuses more on the importance of ground fighting. The ultimate objective of this strategy is adapting a dominant position with effective scrambles and implementing a wide range of finishing techniques.

Similar to other martial arts, BJJ firmly bases its principles on tradition, respect, and honor. Therefore, beginners need to leave any overconfident and egoistic nature at home when attending classes.

Also, note that the only acceptable means to overcome your struggles in Brazilian Jiu-Jitsu is to practice humility. Be humble and listen intently to what your coaches teach, and you may also want to seek advice from your more experienced and skilled teammates.

Preparing for Your First Brazilian Jiu-Jitsu Class

The key for beginners to be able to overcome the initial training difficulties in Brazilian Jiu-Jitsu is to be fully prepared for the first session. Anyone serious about learning and mastering BJJ may experience unpleasant sweaty hands and some butterflies in their stomach, especially if they are still unsure of what to expect when they walk through the doors of their chosen academy for the first time.

Many Brazilian Jiu-Jitsu schools allow new and potential students to watch a class first. You can meet an instructor, giving you the chance to ask some questions before you begin training. Some schools even provide a trial class, allowing aspiring BJJ students to decide whether they really want to push ahead with the actual classes and training.

What Should You Wear?

As a beginner, you do not have to invest in a BJJ Gi during your trial class or the first session. A t-shirt or rash guard and a pair of board shorts will be okay. However, ensure that you don't wear clothing with pockets, baggy fabrics, or belt loops, as they may put you in danger, especially if they catch your toes and fingers.

Wearing a pair of flip-flops instead of shoes is also advisable, as no shoes are worn on the mat. If, after a trial session, you decide to go ahead with BJJ, purchasing a Gi must be a priority and should be worn to all classes.

The traditional BJJ uniform needs a belt to keep the jacket in place. The belt is also used for some defensive or offensive positions, which you'll learn as you train. Belts also represent your rank as a Brazilian Jiu-Jitsu martial artist. You'll also need grappling shorts, which don't slide easily and give you much-needed flexibility on the ground. A rash guard is always a good idea as it can absorb moisture and keep your body cool during training sessions and actual matches. You'll definitely have to get a mouth guard despite BJJ not having kicks or punches, but it's worn for safety in case you fall head-first or an accident happens during training.

You might want to get groin protectors as that area is highly exposed in BJJ and could suffer an injury. Headgear or ear protectors are used to protect the head and ears. The head is pulled during games, which could lead to serious ear injuries; in particular, cauliflower ear is a common BJJ injury. As a beginner, it's recommended that you get knee pads and braces as you'll likely fall and may land on your knees.

Hygiene

Proper hygiene is also a must before setting foot into your first class. Ensure that your toenails and fingernails are properly groomed. If your hair is long, style it into a bun or a ponytail during the class. Take out any piercings and remove any jewelry to avoid injuries. Generally speaking, you need to keep clean because no one really wants to train with an untidy partner. You need to ensure you're the kind of person people want to train with. Ensure your uniform is always clean and your breath is fresh to avoid alienating training partners and making the experience bad for others.

What to Expect During the First Class?

Since it is your first time attending the BJJ class, it is advisable to arrive at class early. If possible, go to the school or academy 5 to 10 minutes ahead of your scheduled class. This way, you will have time to introduce yourself to your instructor. If you have not visited the school yet, you may use those extra minutes to check out what is available.

Also, note that you may be required to sign an indemnity form before taking your first or trial class. Before the class starts, dress appropriately for the training and do some stretching to prepare your body.

Each training session will also start with a lineup, so expect this during your first time attending the class. Note that this lineup is not the classic or traditional one often implemented in kickboxing classes. In BJJ, groups are split based on experience levels and belts. Since you are still a beginner who may not have either, you will line up at the end, where the beginners' group is situated.

Warm-Up Sessions

Your first BJJ class will teach you the importance of warming up. The warm-up session is similar to the ones implemented in other sports. However, if you don't consider conditioning as your strength or forte, avoid rushing it. It would benefit you to keep your energy level for what comes next.

Also, note that since you are still a beginner, there is a possibility that you will spend more of your time watching and observing your instructor as they demonstrate basic BJJ techniques and the logic behind each one. During this initial stage, you will most likely learn the following ground positions:

- Ground (open, closed, and half-guard positions)
- Full and back mounts
- Side control

Some instructors will let you do light warm-ups, while others begin their classes with heavy-duty conditioning. Some classes also begin with a warm-up that is done in groups, like push-ups and running laps. Expect these group warm-ups to be followed by solo drills, such as backward and forward break-falls and shrimping.

Some moves may be very new to you, but don't fret. Watch and observe what others are doing and copy them. Your goal is to learn ways to fall to the ground safely. Also, as a beginner, be lenient with yourself. Do not be too harsh on yourself if you have a hard time doing the exercises and training correctly at first.

Remember that no one can get everything right on their first day. It requires much practice. With discipline and perseverance, you will eventually receive a higher belt. Your instructor will teach you how to correctly do the BJJ moves and techniques.

What to Look for in a BJJ Instructor

Finding the right BJJ instructor is one of the most important steps on your Black Belt journey. Without the right teacher, you could easily get frustrated or seriously injure yourself. A good instructor will push you to improve, and you'll want to, but at the same time, they won't be so overbearing and obnoxious that you wouldn't enjoy the experience. At the end of the day, hard and challenging as the sport may be, you should enjoy yourself and have a good time with your BJJ classes. Here's what you need to look for in a BJJ instructor.

Knowledge and Abilities: The first thing you want in your BJJ instructor is technical knowledge. They don't need to be a world champion or anything, just someone who has practiced the sport long enough to know what they're doing. You need to remember that champions don't necessarily make for good coaches. In fact, in many cases, they don't. You need a Brazilian Jiu-Jitsu coach who has the necessary knowledge about the fundamentals of the sport and the specifics of the techniques. The instructor's current knowledge isn't the only thing to keep in mind, but also, how willing are they to learn and grow? The last thing that you need is a rigid teacher who is unwilling to learn, let alone teach, new moves.

The question is, how do you know if your teacher has good technical knowledge and abilities? Try a class or two with them and observe how they do things. If your teacher just does moves quickly without taking the time to explain the details of every move and why they did it like that, chances are their technical knowledge isn't very good, and they don't have much to teach you. A knowledgeable instructor will let you know how everything is done and how you can replicate those moves. They will take the time to explain the tiniest details and answer any question you might have.

Level of Care: The last thing that you need is a BJJ instructor who doesn't even pay attention to what you're doing in the class. It can be common to find the head coach just walking around the school, watching students go about their techniques, making a remark here or there. This is not a good approach to learning Jiu-Jitsu. You need hands-on experience, a coach who will step into the ring and help you learn and grow, not sit on the sidelines checking their social media. Your BJJ instructor needs to be active and involved in your training. It's also a sign of respect for the sport and you; respect always has and always will be a cornerstone of martial arts.

You're paying a lot of money for your classes, so the head coach should also be the one training you. Make sure they're not pawning you off to some inexperienced instructor still learning the ropes. Moreover, the level of care you get in the school is shown in their teaching style. Is there a fixed curriculum, or are they just doing things without a proper course to follow? You need to have a plan with end goals to monitor and assess your progress. Winging it is not the way to go regarding martial arts. A fixed plan followed with all new students ensures that you deal with professionals who know what they're doing.

Communication Skills: A good teacher is a good communicator, whether with sciences or martial arts. Teaching BJJ doesn't just require physical skills but also verbal ones. How good is your instructor at delivering their point and explaining their intended meaning? Are they clear in their instructions? An instructor may have all the technical knowledge and experience in the world, but if they can't effectively deliver that information, they are not benefitting their students. The instructor's body language makes a difference, too. How approachable are they? Do they feel like the kind of person you can approach with questions and concerns? You don't really want to be training with a confrontational BJJ instructor who is not open to questions. You also don't want to be taught by someone who doesn't like what they're doing and can't wait to get the classes over.

This brings us to patience, the quality you need the most in your BJJ instructor. Getting better in this sport takes a long time, and you will struggle at first to learn new moves and understand new techniques. You need a patient instructor who will give you the space you need to learn. Many instructors seem to forget how scary it can be to begin something new, especially martial arts, and they can show frustration at their students' inability to grasp the terms and the moves. This naturally reflects on your own feelings as a student, and you begin to feel their frustration. If you find that your instructor is impatient from the get-go, you need to find another. A patient instructor can help you learn and give you a safe space to do so. Their patience also affects higher-belt students, who will be just as patient as their teacher with lower-belt novices. This creates a healthy environment for students of all belts to grow and learn together without being rushed. It also creates a powerful bond between you and your instructor, which is very hard to break.

Conduct: A good BJJ instructor carries themselves outside of the ring just as well as inside. You need to find a qualified instructor who is also a decent person. As you'll explore in this book, Brazilian Jiu-Jitsu -- like many martial arts -- is about humbling yourself and letting go of your ego. It's about being honorable and kind. This is why the coach's behavior outside the ring is just as important. You don't want to be taught by someone who happens to be an abuser or a bully who uses his martial arts knowledge to terrorize the weak. You might think the separation between their teaching abilities and conduct is possible - but it isn't - and before you know it, you might turn into them and misuse your newly learned abilities.

Make sure you read online about a coach and see what other former students say about their behavior. If some former students or parents say that the instructor is abusive or a bully, stay away from them. If you can't find much about the coach online, take a few classes with them and see if the school's culture and the instructor's attitude suit you before deciding to continue or find another.

First Few BJJ Techniques

After warming up, your instructor may partner you with someone. Also, similar to other beginners in their first lesson, you may have to stay at the side of the mat to observe and practice basic BJJ techniques. But, there will be instances when you will be combined with the class.

Some schools let you practice BJJ based on their beginner curriculum, while others require you to learn the techniques taught on the day you first attend the class. A few basic techniques you will most likely learn during your first BJJ class are the scissor sweep, mount escape, side control and escape, and guard pass.

If you are included in the primary class, inform your partner that it is your first lesson. Your partner will then know to take things slowly, guide you, and inform you accordingly.

After your first class, reflect on your overall experience to decide whether you should push through with the training. If you choose to continue, discuss membership fees and availability of classes; also, you'll need to obtain a Gi. You can buy your BJJ Gi from most instructors and legit online and martial arts stores.

Essential Tips for Brazilian Jiu-Jitsu Beginners

Since you have decided to go through with the training, you have to arm yourself with valuable tips other than those you learned during your first class. Guiding yourself with additional useful tips will lessen the somewhat intimidating feeling of learning the art of Brazilian Jiu-Jitsu.

Commit to Training Consistently

Obviously, consistent training is vital to succeeding in mastering Brazilian Jiu-Jitsu. While there is no guarantee that you will participate in each training session, especially if there are emergencies, you still have to stick to a consistent approach in training. It is the key to developing your skills while keeping up with developments within the class.

For example, if your instructor teaches a specific technique, position, or move for at least a week and you only take part in the class towards the end, it will be harder to put together the entirety of the session.

So, commit to practice and repetition, and you will notice a significant improvement in your entire performance.

Train at least twice or three times every week and, if possible, take on additional training, too - staying after class for additional roles, attending open mats, and working on solo drills once you are at home. You may also want to coordinate with your team members so you can roll even during those times when the gym is not open. Extra practice will be enough for you to notice steady progress in your Brazilian Jiu-Jitsu performance.

Ask Questions

As a beginner, you will have many questions regarding the practice of Brazilian Jiu-Jitsu. Do not hesitate or be afraid to ask whatever question is on your mind during classes. If you don't raise your questions, you may have a difficult time mastering this new activity.

Luckily, most senior members, coaches, or instructors will always be around to answer your questions and concerns about BJJ. You may have to wait for the Q&A portion, which often happens at the end of every class or training to raise your concerns.

Also, make it a point to pick up hints from others with more experience after each training session. Your classmates will be more than willing to offer what they know about this sport, and you can ask them to give you honest opinions regarding your performance.

This way, you will know your mistakes and the specific areas you should improve. All these details play a crucial role in your performance and will certainly help your progress.

Arrive Early

Another crucial tip for Brazilian Jiu-Jitsu beginners is to get to class as early as possible, or at least 10 minutes before your scheduled class. It gives you sufficient time to change, loosen up and step onto your mat for a quick warm-up session.

If, for some reason, you run late for a session, let your instructor or coach know about your arrival. A quick apology for your tardiness is a must, and get onto the mat without delay. Regardless of what you do, avoid slipping onto your mat unnoticed because this may disrupt the entire class's training.

Keep Your Fingernails and Toenails Short

You must keep your fingernails and toenails short when attending Brazilian Jiu-Jitsu classes to ensure no injuries from you or your training partners during sparring or drilling. This is not an exaggeration, as long fingernails and toenails can cause damage during each of your BJJ sessions, and some even have scars as proof of the damage caused by long nails.

Moreover, your fingernails are home to plenty of bacteria, which may cause cuts to become infected. So, make it a point to ensure your nails are trimmed prior to attending class. It is also good hygiene.

Master Fundamental Movements First

It's imperative as a beginner to avoid attempting complex movements before you ever master the fundamentals. As a White Belt holder (a new Brazilian Jiu-Jitsu student), you must focus on learning and mastering the fundamentals to prepare you for more complex actions later. You should initially focus on some fundamental movements: shrimping, bridging, sweeping, and getting up.

- **Bridging** - Lie on your back and raise both your knees, keeping your legs at a 90-degree bend, forming the shape of a bridge by raising your hips.

- **Shrimping** - This movement is about mobility even when you are on your back, requiring you to use your hips and shoulders as if they are feet to move around conveniently.

- **Sweeping** - In this BJJ move, you use both your feet to take out your opponent's legs and base. The result of this movement is enforcing a better ground position to increase your chance of winning.

- **Getting Up** - Of course, this involves moving to a standing position. However, it is important to stick to a technical stand-up, as the most vital aspect is ensuring you never compromise your head.

Shrimping and bridging are two of the most vital movements connecting all other moves and techniques together. It is also crucial to perfect bridging before learning and understanding the basics of escaping a bad and unwanted position. Moreover, you must develop shrimping on both sides and improve your ability to get up and complete a sweep before you can finally try more advanced and complex submissions and positions. By honing your skills in these fundamentals and connecting them smoothly, you will significantly mark your advancement as a beginner (white belt holder).

Relax When Rolling

Another essential tip for Brazilian Jiu-Jitsu beginners is to let go of nervousness, anxiety, and tension during your first roll. The first time you have to conduct rolling is also your first chance to put everything you have practiced and learned into action.

Remember, you are still in the initial stage of your journey, so your understanding and knowledge about this position may be limited. But, it is not a reason to feel nervous and tense during your first attempt at rolling. Let go of these emotions by accepting that you are still a beginner, as all you can do right now is go with the flow.

You may also want to take this chance to try new things - making mistakes and taking some risks. Learn how to relax your body before making this move, and remain comfortable throughout, as this is the key to multiple rolls and speeding up your learning process.

Train for Strength and Endurance

Integrate some strength and endurance training into your routines. You need these skills to perform Brazilian Jiu-Jitsu moves more effectively and easily. There is no need to turn yourself into a powerlifter or long-distance runner. You merely have to train for strength and endurance to get into the best shape for BJJ and avoid injuries.

Do Not Bring Your Ego to Your BJJ Classes

It would be best for you to leave your ego at home. If your goal for training is to prove that you are good at something, then maybe you should stop now. Remember, as a beginner, you will only evolve in this martial art form if you train with humility and without your egotistical personality. You will achieve better results if you train while keeping your mind open.

Here are some points to remember during training so that you can continue practicing with humility and an open mind:

- You can never expect to learn everything, especially if you are only starting.

- Avoid hurting yourself by patting as many times as needed.

- Avoid forcing a position if your partner says he does not want to. For instance, if he does not like to palm, avoid forcing him to do it. You can't benefit from it, and it may only hurt your partner.

- Do not beat yourself up when you make mistakes. Allow yourself these mistakes every now and then, and learn more from your mistakes.

- Receive every piece of advice about BJJ with an open mind.

Never let your ego exist during your training. Otherwise, you may bruise it, causing you to stop training. To succeed in BJJ, humility is a must, and you must keep your head down and commit to training hard.

Speaking of humility, make it your goal to become a better version of yourself rather than others when it comes to BJJ training. The philosophy behind martial arts, in general, isn't about surpassing others but yourself. This isn't just a lesson in humility but a way to keep steady progress without suffering setbacks and frustration. The surest way to hinder your own progress is to compare yourself to others. We all have our different journeys, and yours is special and unique. Looking at what others are doing and comparing yourself will only bring you down. The people you're comparing yourself to might have freer schedules to practice or are natural athletes. The competition you put yourself in with them is pointless and won't work in your favor, so don't start one in the first place.

Your soul goal should be to work on your own skills and improve, regardless of other people's progress. Discipline yourself to focus on your own progress. Rather than ask if you could defeat your classmate, ask if you can beat yourself from a few weeks ago. This will help you stop worrying about whether or not your classmates are better. It doesn't matter; the only thing that matters is your own progress.

Patience and Persistence

They're your only hope if you want to get better at BJJ. This type of martial arts is an art form; like any other art form, it takes time to master. This isn't about natural talent or skills. It's about who can persist and endure the grueling training process to get better with each passing day. The thing about martial arts is they build a powerful work ethic because every inch of progress you make is hard-earned through tears, sweat, and probably blood. This makes the whole journey very satisfying, but you just need to be patient and trust the process.

BJJ has a very high dropout rate because many beginners feel frustrated when they start training. It looks and feels hard, and, normally, you would feel this is something you'll never be able to do well. You can spend months training and still feel like you're not going anywhere, which is also normal. However, this is not the case. You are getting better, and there is progress. You just can't see it. Those who plow through the negative emotions and frustration will, though. One day sparring with your classmate, you will feel stronger and more confident, and you'll win. Becoming skilled in Brazilian Jiu-Jitsu takes years, and it's not something that will happen after a couple of months of training.

It helps along this journey if you set short and long-term goals. Yes, you need to progress at your own pace, but that doesn't mean you shouldn't have long-term goals and hopes. You shouldn't aspire to get the Blue Belt but the Black Belt. It might seem far now, but the more you work and put in the hours, the closer this goal becomes.

Tap Out

One of the most important lessons you must remember as you train to become a BJJ martial artist is that there is no shame in tapping out. This isn't to say that you should surrender easily or quit whenever it gets tough, but it's important to learn when you've lost and tap out. This is a very common mistake for many beginners who are simply unwilling to tap out. While a fighting spirit is commendable in BJJ and something you should keep, not knowing when to tap out can lead to serious injuries and complicate your journey before it even starts.

Remember that the goal of training is to get better and improve. You have nothing to prove to anyone. It's not about winning or losing at this point in your BJJ journey. You have to train yourself to forego the traditional notions of winning and losing because they serve you no good. When you tap out, there's always something to learn. Don't think of it as a loss but rather as a learning opportunity. As you get better, you will learn the necessary techniques to help you get out of chokes and submission attempts, but until then, stay safe and learn when it is time to tap out.

Common Beginner Mistakes in Brazilian Jiu-Jitsu

You can make the most of your BJJ classes if you are aware of common mistakes. This section discusses common BJJ beginner mistakes.

Not Learning Appropriate Grip

Grappling against an opponent requires you to get a hold of them. Many beginners are unaware of the significance of correctly making a proper handgrip, and it is something you must master if you want to succeed in BJJ. There are three vital components for an effective grip which are hand strength, the exact place where you should grip, and efficient gripping.

Hand strength is essential in Jiu-Jitsu, so it is necessary to properly train the muscles in both hands to improve hand strength. A few exercises are meant to make your hands stronger, including kettlebell swings, rope pulls, rope climbs, using claw-hold weights and pinch-hold weights.

It is also crucial to learn how to do an efficient grip because no matter how excellent your hand strength is, an inefficient grip will still cause your forearms to weaken, resulting in the loss of your grip. Among the handgrips you need to master as a beginner, include the following:

- **Pistol Grip** - Grab onto the BJJ Gi using your pinky closest to your opponent's wrist. Ensure that you are grabbing a lot of the material. The grip is the same as when you hold the handle of a pistol.

- **C-Grip** - Use four fingers and curl your thumb inward, similar to when forming the letter C, to grab your opponent, usually at the arm or wrist.

- **Spider Grip** - In this grip, you have to use four fingers, curling inwards to grab your opponent's GI sleeve.

- **Monkey Grip** - Grab using the topmost parts of the joints of your four fingers.

Another vital element to gripping is the exact spot where you should grip in order to obtain the best leverage.

If you have no idea about the exact places where you should grip, you will be unable to gain leverage regardless of how secure you think your grip is. To give you an idea, the perfect spots to grip include the pants, cuffs, lapels, and the ends of the collar sleeve.

Not Focusing on the Basics

Some beginners in Brazilian Jiu-Jitsu are so excited to move on to more complex and advanced techniques that they neglect the importance of honing their basic skills. As a white belt, you may also be tempted to learn everything at once. However, do your best to avoid making this common mistake.

Make it a point to perfect the basic moves in Jiu-Jitsu and be patient along the process. You will eventually reward yourself with a much better experience when you move on to more complex techniques.

- **Side Control Escape** - This famous move allows you to effectively move your hips starting from the bottom, and it is also the most basic move you can perform for a great escape.

- **Triangle Choke** - This signature move is for submission. It is a basic move that you have to master as you will have to use it when dealing with an opponent who is bigger than you.

- **Scissor Sweep** - This is another basic move you should master, as every sweep technique is based on this sweep. Using the scissor sweep will cause your opponent to lose his balance to your advantage. It would be best to use the scissor sweep together with other basic moves for the best results.

- **Cross Collar Choke** - This grip serves as your starting point before you do any sweep or attack.

- **Americana Lock** - This basic move refers to a common lock used when grappling an opponent. Performed correctly, you can take complete control of your opponent's arm.

- **Hip Bump Sweep** – Master this sweep technique as you will use it once your opponent is already down on his knees.

Never ignore the importance of learning these basic moves, and you can become one of the best Brazilian Jiu-Jitsu masters.

Neglecting the Importance of Self-Defense

Never overlook the importance of learning a few self-defense techniques. Some beginners make this mistake and consequently cannot get out of a simple choke because they do not know basic self-defense.

Instead of neglecting self-defense, continuously go over the essentials you learned at the start of your training. Once you have mastered them, you will know how to rehash them and turn them into a defense tactic.

Holding onto a Submission or Position for Too Long

One of the things you will learn when practicing Brazilian Jiu-Jitsu for the first time is the perfect time to let go when you're in a position that does not work for you.

As a BJJ beginner, you should master how to move to the cross choke after posing for the mount for too long – when the opponent already knows how to protect himself. The faster you master the art of recognizing when to let go, the faster you will improve your Brazilian Jiu-Jitsu skills.

Not Knowing Your Physical Limits

If you are serious about mastering Brazilian Jiu-Jitsu, then learn how to train wisely. In their attempt to learn and master this martial art quickly, some beginners force themselves to train twice a day, six days a week. Ultimately, this is not wise and may only cause burnout.

Once you reach a burned-out stage, you may feel the need to stop training for a while, defeating your purpose of mastering it. Instead of burning yourself out, stick to the average training frequency of twice or three times every week. Keep in mind that BJJ is not a sprint, so learn slowly but surely.

Probably the most important of all the tips that Brazilian Jiu-Jitsu beginners must know is to have fun. Trust the entire process, and do not forget to enjoy the entire experience. Avoid holding a completion after three taps. If you are in doubt whether your partner tapped, just let go. It would be much better for you to be cautious than to have to deal with discomfort.

Trust your coaches, instructors, and partners, too. You will make the environment where you are training look and feel safer, resulting in a much more enjoyable and fun experience learning this martial art.

Chapter 3: The Basics of Grappling in BJJ: How Not to Get Bullied in a Fight

In One-on-one combat, grappling involves seizing or gripping an opponent at a close range as a means of getting a significant physical edge or advantage. Fighters do this by imposing a solid position. Grappling encompasses many disciplines – among them are those followed by Brazilian Jiu-Jitsu participants.

The term grappling involves techniques used in many combat sports, particularly martial arts and Brazilian Jiu-Jitsu. Successful grappling means that you effectively apply counters and maneuvers to your opponent, giving you a better position and physical advantage.

It also covers techniques designed to force your opponents to submit. However, remember that grappling will never involve using weapons, and you should never strike your opponent when applying the grappling technique.

Importance of Grappling in BJJ

Brazilian Jiu-Jitsu's main focus will always be on ground grappling. You must master grappling techniques as it is the key to taking your opponents down to the ground and forcing submissions through triangle choke techniques.

Ground grappling includes all grappling styles and techniques that you apply when you are no longer standing. The most important part of implementing this technique is proper positioning. You must be in a dominant position, which is often characterized as on top of your opponent.

In this dominant position, you have plenty of options on what you can do next. You may attempt to escape by standing up, striking your opponent, performing a submission hold, or obtaining a hold-down or pin with the end goal of exhausting and controlling your opponent. Meanwhile, expect the bottom grappler to focus more on how to escape and improve his position. In this case, they may use a reversal or sweep.

Mastering grappling techniques should be one of your ultimate goals when learning and mastering Brazilian Jiu-Jitsu to control your opponents and defeat them. Many martial artists even make it a point to learn a few submission techniques and counters to ensure that they can integrate a ground element into their usual, traditional training.

It would be best to practice and hone your knowledge and skills about grappling under the supervision of a martial arts instructor. That way, you can avoid injuries and ensure that you learn and master the correct techniques.

Grappling Classifications

Grappling is an effective means to improve your endurance and strength to prevent being bullied by your attacker. It involves the use of various muscle groups and maximizes their efficiency. Aside from muscle-building, grappling techniques also offer cardiovascular benefits while boosting your mental focus. These are all vital skills required in intense BJJ physical training.

The good thing about grappling is that you can also use it in self-defense. By mastering grappling techniques, you can use one or two to protect yourself from attackers successfully. There are limitless possibilities and variations in grappling to reach a takedown and seize and control your opponent. Also, take note of the following classifications of Brazilian Jiu-Jitsu:

- **Clinching** - Also called clinch work, this grappling classification occurs when both fighters are on their feet using a wide range of clinch holds directed to the opponent's upper body. Clinching is often used as a means of setting up or defending against takedowns or throws.

- **Takedown** - A takedown is the effective manipulation of an opponent to bring them to the ground from a standing position. Your goal for the takedown is to get into a dominant position.

- **Throw** - This grappling technique involves lifting the opponent or putting them off-balance, so you can forcefully maneuver them to the ground. The main objective of throws differs from one discipline to another, but the thrower can get into a controlling position, obtain a takedown, or leave them standing.

- **Submission Holds** - There are two types of submission holds - the choke, which potentially requires strangling or suffocating your opponent, and the lock, which requires injuring a joint or any part of the body. If you perform a submission hold and your opponent can no longer escape, expect them to submit by tapping or even verbally indicating their acceptance of defeat. A fighter who refuses or fails to tap out is at risk of incurring a serious injury or becoming unconscious.

- **Sprawling** - This is a defensive grappling technique you can use if your opponent tries to perform a takedown. Shift your legs backward, then spread them out in a single, rapid motion. The correct execution of sprawling results in your opponents landing on their back, giving you complete control.

- **Controlling or Securing Techniques** - One technique that falls under this classification is a pin, which you can do by holding your opponent on the back. The pin forces your opponent into a position where they can no longer attack.

Some competitive grappling styles consider the successful execution of a pin as an immediate victory. Other styles consider it a dominant position that awards the athlete several points.

Aside from the pin, there are other controlling and securing techniques, like holding your opponent face down or on all fours, preventing them from attacking or escaping. All these techniques, when successfully performed, lead to a submission hold.

- **Escape** - This grappling classification is when you maneuver yourself out of a dangerous or inferior position. For example, when the grappler, who is beneath an opponent, controls movements sideways to guard or successfully returns to a standing position considered neutral. Also, when the grappler escapes from a submission attempt and returns to a position, that lowers the submission hold risk.

- **Turnover** - The turnover is used to control your opponent, particularly when they are on all fours, prepare for a pin, or get into a dominant position. You will score valuable points with a turnover.

- **Sweep or Reversal** - This grappling technique is when a grappler maneuvers the position beneath their opponent while on the ground. The goal of the sweep or reversal is to obtain a top position.

Grappling Styles and Techniques

Apart from the major classifications of grappling already mentioned, some other styles and techniques are also perfectly suitable for Brazilian Jiu-Jitsu.

Leg Trip

This method requires you to use your leg to force your opponent off balance and bring them to the ground. This technique is further subdivided into two - the single and the double leg trip.

The single-leg takedown - grab one leg of your opponent using both your hands. The goal here is to bring your opponent to the ground by pulling the lower part of the leg using your shoulder.

Single leg takedowns also come in several types; the ankle lift, which requires you to pick up the leg by the ankle, and the high crotch, which requires you to pull up your opponent's leg by the crotch area. Using either technique, you can attack the leg across or away from the body.

The Double-Leg Takedown

Grab the legs of your opponent using both arms. Keep your chest closer to your opponent's leg, and force them to the ground, which is the ultimate goal of grappling.

Other skills to force your opponent to the ground include slamming, pulling the legs, and pushing them forward using your shoulders.

Ankle Pinch Takedown

This style is perhaps one of the best techniques adopted by Brazilian Jiu-Jitsu. Push the head of your opponent over one knee. Your goal is to immobilize your opponent's leg. Complete the ankle pinch takedown by stepping inward and blocking the targeted foot before grabbing the ankle. Then lift your opponent's foot, causing them to fall.

Triangle Choke

This is an iconic and popular BJJ submission hold. Many fighters use the triangle choke from the guard. However, it is a very versatile technique that can be done in many ways.

Use your legs to trap your opponent's neck and one arm.

The pressure of your thigh across your opponent's neck disrupts blood flow. It is a very effective technique as the opponent will most likely tap out, signifying their acceptance of defeat.

Rear Naked Choke

This is another popular submission hold used by grapplers in BJJ. Exert pressure on your opponent's head's blood circulation, making them uncomfortable and prone to unconsciousness unless they tap out.

This technique also usually follows a back mount, which requires you to wrap your arm around the neck of your opponents. Use your opposite arm to grab or take hold of your opponent's biceps. Apply pressure to the designated area using the strength and force of your biceps.

Using your free hand, put pressure on the back of your opponent's head, deepening the choke.

Guard

Trap your opponent between your legs. You can open or lock this position using your ankles. The guard is designed to force your opponent to break the stronghold of their posture, tiring them out. You can also consider the guard a defense strategy requiring strikes.

Closed Guard

The closed guard is a crucial concept in grappling with many variations. Expect the closed guard to be one of the first guards you will learn as a white belt or BJJ beginner.

Lock your opponent between your legs by crossing your feet behind their back. A significant advantage of the closed guard is that you have the opportunity for submission or sweep simultaneously.

Note there is no one superior technique with guards as it depends on the situation. Aside from the closed guard, the other variations are half guard, X guard, butterfly, and open guard.

Technical Mount

The mount is another powerful position for those wanting to make the most out of grappling. However, it's essential to understand everything about this move and position so you can maximize its full advantage.

While some find it overrated, it is an extremely important move you can use once you reach more advanced BJJ levels. It is a useful counter technique allowing you to maintain a reasonable and excellent position for an attack.

Importance of Stretching and Flexibility

Undeniably, Brazilian Jiu-Jitsu is a sport that is physically and mentally demanding. Grappling alone has many techniques, variations, and positions that require you to move various parts of your body unconventionally. It is the primary reason you must learn more about stretching and flexibility, as both have crucial roles in improving your grappling technique performance.

Stretching and flexibility help you stay healthy while keeping you free of injuries as you continue with your training. Moreover, including stretching in your BJJ training assures you of a balanced and long-term program.

Depending on your game plan and your unique grappling style, your flexibility level will either be lower or higher than that of your opponent. Understanding your flexibility level enables you to control and force your opponent to submit.

You must be familiar with the different stretching techniques to succeed in BJJ. These techniques will improve your flexibility, leading you to better performance.

Active Stretching

Active stretching techniques refer to exercises that allow you to move your joints actively using various motions. It is ideal to do active stretching as part of your warm-up exercises before BJJ class or conditioning. You can also use active stretching as a component of an independent mobility routine, which you perform separately from other training, like in the morning after your rest day or when you wake up.

Some warm-up exercises designed explicitly for BJJ, like shrimping and bridges, can be classified as active stretching, provided you do them while consciously exerting effort in executing a full range of movement.

Passive Stretching

Stretching techniques and exercises are considered passive if they involve moving your joints to their flexibility tolerance. Hold the specific position when you experience mild discomfort for at least 20 seconds. It encompasses external assistance, like a BJJ belt, as a means of stretching your hamstrings.

Just like the active stretches, you can also do the passive ones independently at the end of mobility routines. Perform the passive stretches after your BJJ training, preferably within five to ten minutes after the session, as it is also when you have an elevated body temperature.

Passive stretching performed *after* your workout also helps improve your flexibility or range of motion, provided it's done consistently.

What Muscle Groups and Joints Should You Stretch Regularly?

Now that you are familiar with stretching and its importance in boosting your flexibility, it is important to know what specific muscle groups and joints to stretch to improve your BJJ performance. Regularly stretching the right muscle groups and joints improves your strength, which can make you even more effective in grappling.

Ankles

To master BJJ, you need to improve the mobility and flexibility of your ankles to execute techniques correctly and prevent injuries during training and competitions. Note that tight calf muscles can also cause stiff ankles and may cause limitations in flexing your foot.

Rearward tension in your feet is necessary when executing strong butterfly hooks and proof that you must improve the mobility of your ankles with controlled rotations. If your calf tightens, then you may want to do static calf stretches.

Hips

It is essential for Brazilian Jiu-Jitsu fighters to improve their hip mobility (to prevent injury), and this also helps them to deliver incredible performances. External hip rotations will help you obtain a strong offensive and defensive guard.

Having good hip extension is also helpful whenever you need to escape from a bad position, bridging, completing the submission, or passing guard. Do passive and active stretching techniques that target the glutes, hamstrings, hip rotators, and quads to improve hip mobility.

Upper Back

Also called the T-spine, your upper back must have high flexibility levels to prevent spine and upper back injuries. If you have tight shoulders, lats, and pecs, your upper back likely lacks mobility. BJJ requires many rounded defensive postures, and low flexibility will result in a stiff upper back or T-spine.

Shoulders

Improve the mobility of your shoulders by doing appropriate stretching exercises that target the muscles in this area. With improved shoulder mobility, you can prevent the most common shoulder injuries many grapplers often deal with. Similar to the defensive and rounded posture that triggers stiffness in the T-spine, it also causes immobility or inflexibility to the shoulders.

When and How Often Should You Stretch?

If you want to master grappling, never neglect the importance of stretching consistently. Apart from the muscle groups and joints mentioned, stretch your neck and wrists regularly to improve mobility. It is advisable to perform stretching as frequently as possible, and it is even more important if you have mobility problems. Do your chosen active stretching routines daily as part of your morning rituals.

Focus on passive routines after workouts or before you go to bed. Add a few passive stretching exercises to the active ones, but avoid passive stretching before you do heavy physical activities. It is not highly recommended before strength and conditioning training.

You will notice a significant improvement in your mobility, flexibility, and strength by doing these recommended stretching routines, ultimately executing various grappling techniques without any problems and demonstrating promise as a future dominant BJJ fighter.

Chapter 4: The Law of Action and Reaction

From an outsider's perspective, Brazilian Jiu-Jitsu may get the impression that the entire sport is only about complicated chokeholds and grappling. As a white belt or a beginner with only a few days of training, you may view BJJ in the same way.

You will notice that most moves and techniques require many steps. You feel like effectively mastering and employing them is only possible after many years of practice.

However, as you gain more experience, you gain a deep appreciation of the high level of skill, knowledge, and dedication required to transform yourself into a great BJJ fighter.

Even though you experience difficulties at first, try to grasp everything you're taught during classes. Eventually, you will realize that embracing and understanding the core principles and disciplines of BJJ gives you an edge over others.

Importance of the Principle-based Approach to Learning BJJ

Brazilian Jiu-Jitsu, like other martial arts, relies on its core disciplines and principles. Mastering BJJ is not about mastering each step, technique, or move; it is when you understand its principles and modify them based on various scenarios and opponents.

While still recognizing the principles, theories, and disciplines of BJJ, you can add a few personal touches to demonstrate your own artistry level. It is safe to say that the principle-based approach to mastering BJJ differs a lot from the memory-based one.

Remember, while memorizing each move is essential to learn Brazilian Jiu-Jitsu's basics, it may hinder growth. The reason is that committing certain moves to memory may also indicate that you lack the inherent comprehension of its core principles.

This can be disadvantageous, especially when an unfamiliar move performed by your opponent catches you off-guard. To help with this, beginners (white belts) must work with different partners, as it helps to reimagine various fight scenarios.

It is a fantastic opportunity to put the moves you learned in class into practice in the real world. It also helps you understand the underlying theories that make the movements effective.

Core Principles and Disciplines of BJJ and Other Martial Arts

As mentioned earlier, Brazilian Jiu-Jitsu is a martial art that focuses on grappling and that uses leverage principles. The focus of BJJ is always on positional control, takedowns, submissions, and grappling, and this is an effective means to improve every modality of fitness, like agility, mobility, and core strength.

Mentally, you can liken Brazilian Jiu-Jitsu to a chess game, as tactical thinking is the correct strategy and will contribute to success. When you are on the training ground or in your class, it is important to show that you have a solid grasp of the fundamental principles and disciplines of BJJ. Some of the essential principles and disciplines of BJJ, and other martial arts, are covered in this section.

Zen Stage

The Zen stage is a vital principle that allows fighters to learn and understand Brazilian Jiu-Jitsu. The principles valorize the significance of repetition. Note that repeating a Jiu-Jitsu technique several times over many years may lead to you executing the BJJ technique *without even thinking about it.*

It is even possible for your muscle memory to do the BJJ technique as if on autopilot in the same way as habits are formed. Therefore, you must apply proper repetition to enjoy its varied benefits, including - but not limited to - what's listed here.

- **Perfect the Technique** - This builds a strong base for all moves, no matter how different. You will also gain a solid foundation to improve your strength, the overall quality of execution, and movement sequences.

- **Puts Your Mind at a Phase of Emptiness** - this is needed for more effective execution of your moves and techniques

- **Becomes a Habit** - Drilling a BJJ technique repeatedly and correctly turns it into a habit. Humans are creatures of habit, so what you do repeatedly makes up who you are. So, if you improve your habits, expect to improve your performance when competing.

However, you must be extra careful when repeating a particular technique incorrectly because repeating it too often will develop incorrect and unwanted habits. Work with a good Brazilian Jiu-Jitsu instructor capable of pointing out your mistakes and guiding you toward developing good and healthy habits.

Balance

In the martial arts world, especially in Brazilian Jiu-Jitsu, a core concept is the principle of balance - not too little nor too much. This specific principle is useful in martial arts training in regard to various aspects of your everyday life, your body, and your emotions.

BJJ fighters - and any other martial artist - perceive balance as not moving or acting too slowly or too fast, meaning that you should not be too tentative or too aggressive, or too low, high, right, or left. It's imperative to practice the principle of balance to control your timing and pace. You must learn to rely on your balance if you want to succeed in BJJ and other martial art forms.

Balance also helps filter your mindset while training. By fully understanding the principle of balance, you accept that your training days will not always be good, and you will experience bad days. So, avoid becoming too frustrated or impatient because of your unrealistic expectations that each training day will be good.

Developing this principle is also key to freeing your mind from depending on the outcome of a specific training session. Instead of doing that, focus on the training's practical process and recognize that attaining balance is also needed by accepting both good and bad days.

You can turn your training session into one that balances your body, emotions, and mind and contribute to delivering an excellent physical performance.

Natural Order

To become a successful BJJ fighter, you must have a complete grasp of the principle related to the natural order. This specific process is about understanding the progressive and continuous changes and development, so prepare for them instead of evading them.

Progression in BJJ and other martial arts will always be equal to concentration and time. It requires spending minimal time to achieve similar progress if your focus is on intensity, but you still have to retain the balance. Also, forcing yourself to train too intensely and for an extended period will only lead to overtraining or burnout. In some cases, your body will be incapable of recovering properly from stress.

However, insufficient training and lack of passion in this martial art form may also result in you failing to attain your goals. So, it is crucial to maintain balance and adhere to the natural order.

One sign that you have attained the correct balance in your attitude towards your BJJ training is when you are genuinely happy with the process. You are also aware that regardless of your BJJ and martial arts achievements, they won't matter that much based on the cosmos' scale and the universal scheme of things.

Action and Reaction

The most important aspect of the many principles and disciplines governing any martial art form is the "action and reaction" principle. In other words, "for every action, expect a reaction."

Brazilian Jiu-Jitsu requires minimal effort to attain maximum results. So, using the action and reaction principle is the best way to achieve success in this sport.

As a beginner still in the learning phase of Brazilian Jiu-Jitsu, there is a chance that your focus is frequently on reacting. You defend submissions or try maintaining your balance and are always on the defense. It's okay as you are still a beginner and learning the ins and outs of the sport.

However, once you begin to learn to defend instinctively, expect your game to change. One significant change is that you spend less brainpower on defense and use more on your intention. For instance, if an attacker is on guard while you throw triangles and set yourself up for the kimura, you may be asking what is running through their mind.

Remember, your attacker is not thinking at that moment – they are reacting. They do not think of the moment passing; they are taking defensive/offensive steps.

Now, think about what will happen if you wait just a little longer to determine their moves. The best possible scenario would be that they will pass your guard. The key to getting a good player to submit is keeping them from a moment of thought.

Importance of Action and Reaction Principle

The action and reaction principle will always be vital in BJJ fighters and martial artists because you can use this principle to set up most of your takedowns and throws.

Attempting to control an opponent who is still standing can be more challenging than fighting on the ground. The reason for this is that your opponent can move freely, react instantly, and escape when standing.

To dissect the meaning of the action and reaction principle, think of your opponent who is about to make a move against you – this is an action. The response (reaction) is when you think and act quickly based on that move, like a counter-attack.

Also, by ensuring that you are aware of the possible defensive reactions of your opponent, you will attack appropriately. Understanding your opponent's best defensive response gives you a chance to equip yourself with knowledge and information to gain more leverage or power. With the action and reaction principle, your strategy is to force a reaction from your opponent, take advantage and react immediately to use their energy to add power and leverage to your moves.

When to Act and React?

Once you know that every attack can provoke a reaction, you will also be smart with your attacks. For instance, you can fake an attack to disguise your real intention and use your opponent's reaction as an opening for your successful technique.

You have to be very observant of the clues that will let you act and react appropriately. Always apply this principle, even when you are no longer in the class. You may lose your belt or even be arrested if you harm someone using the BJJ moves and techniques, whether provoked or not. Therefore, anticipating a person's action and reaction is crucial.

In class, you will realize that the skills associated with acting and reacting at the proper times are due to *repetition.* The more training you undergo, the quicker you will execute the practiced techniques and expect your muscle memory to develop.

When competing and pushing your opponent, expect them to push you back instinctively with similar or increased intensity levels that force the action and reaction principle. Likewise, with pulls, if you intend to pull them forward, push them backward first.

Once your opponent reacts by pushing you, pull them. You will draw on their energy and expend just minimal energy when pulling your opponent forward. You will also do this when implementing the art of reversal (more about this topic later) in your fights.

Taking Advantage of the Action and Reaction Principle

There are several ways to apply this principle, especially when planning to lead your opponent into a different position from that which they planned. Do you intend to sweep them to your left? Then stimulating them to move to your right first is a wise move, as it compromises your opponent's balance. Then decide on your next move based on what happens.

Another way of viewing the action and reaction principle is as bait and trap, meaning luring your opponent so they will react or respond in the way you intended. It helps to react quickly to your opponent's moves so you can make the most of this principle.

For example, if they move their body forward with a specific speed, increase their speed further by pulling them in a similar direction. It may result in your opponent losing their balance, which you can use to your advantage.

The deeper and more experienced you become in Brazilian Jiu-Jitsu, the more you realize that a single move or attack is not as effective when inflicted on more skilled and experienced fighters. You must combine various techniques for the best results when applying the action and reaction principle.

The best way to apply the principle is to analyze what went wrong when a technique failed. Analyze and brainstorm the reaction of your opponents and create your Plan B, which will surely arouse your excitement for your next match, especially if you feel they will prepare a defense against your Plan A.

Chapter 5: Defending Against Attacks: The Art of Reversal

One reason many people become interested in Brazilian Jiu-Jitsu is that it is an excellent form of self-defense. Knowledge about this form of martial art is the key for someone to defend themselves against an attack. Apart from the action and reaction principle, Brazilian Jiu-Jitsu will also help you brush up your knowledge on the art of defense and reversal.

The action and reaction principle has a strong connection to the art of self-defense and reversal that's also a vital part of Brazilian Jiu-Jitsu because you must follow the action and reaction principle to establish a strong defense against an attack. Your defense will be based on your opponent's attack.

What Is Reversal?

Brazilian Jiu-Jitsu reversal is when a player in a disadvantageous position or at the bottom succeeds in reversing their position. The successful reversal will result in the player being in an advantageous or top position. It is a great skill that Brazilian Jiu-Jitsu fighters must master because it gives them the chance to skip a few steps when changing positions every time they initiate the reversal.

A typical change results in the player moving through neutral to good positions after finding themselves in a bad one. Depending on your chosen reversal technique, you can go directly to a good position. The art of reversal is the key to protecting yourself from an attack.

Brazilian Jiu-Jitsu and Self-Defense

Self-defense forms a significant part of BJJ. It is based on the original Japanese Jiu-Jitsu when the Samurai fought for survival; it continues to be a practical fighting system today. All moves taught in BJJ are effective self-defense moves, and some of these techniques are specifically designed for that purpose.

So, it is not surprising that most BJJ schools worldwide pay special attention and focus more on self-defense. In modern Jiu-Jitsu self-defense, strikes do not form part of the system. However, learning the basics of moving around, blocking, and using them is still essential.

It is not that essential to learn and master complex jumping attacks and spinning kicks. Instead, it is better to set simpler goals, like getting close to your attacker or opponent, intending to force submission, or taking them down.

Another thing to remember is that around 90 percent of altercations or fights end with fighters on the ground. People without BJJ skills will be unsure of what to do once they are taken down onto the ground. Your knowledge of Brazilian Jiu-Jitsu can change that, especially with grappling, and it encourages your best techniques.

With your BJJ training, you will know precisely how to defend yourself and remain safe whether you are in the top, back, or bottom position. The self-defense you learn in BJJ will train you to build dominance, even when you are placed in a bad position.

Once you can protect yourself and be in a more dominant position, BJJ will give you an option to do something not offered by other forms of martial art – resolving the situation without harming your opponent or causing an injury. Self-defense in BJJ and several other techniques help you to pin someone down while de-escalating the situation.

On the other hand, you are also allowed to use a submission technique designed to hurt your attacker or opponent when necessary. If you prefer, you can perform strikes. Overall, you won't find other forms of martial arts that are as good for self-defense as BJJ, especially with one-on-one fights or altercations.

Why Is BJJ Perfect for Self-Defense?

Constantly remind yourself that the best weapon for self-defense is your ability to stay away from confrontation. If possible, escape from the situation. However, if the situation reaches the point of becoming physical, make the most of your Brazilian Jiu-Jitsu training to get you out of trouble.

What are the specific reasons why BJJ is good for self-defense?

It Improves Your Comfort Level When Fighting

If you have experienced a situation when someone has tried choking you until you become unconscious, you are probably aware of how uncomfortable it is. Your training will make you feel comfortable with the discomfort and sometimes the pain, and you will deal with the situation automatically.

Unlike striking arts, like Muay Thai, which require sparring for only about 20 percent of the training, Brazilian Jiu-Jitsu involves sparring up to almost 100 percent of the training. Rolling in BJJ is close to an actual fight, though it still does not involve kicking and punching.

Whenever you are in a situation where you are required to protect yourself, you will not be shocked or intimidated by the fighter's physical size due to your sparring training. You will not also experience discomfort when you grapple with someone and take them to the ground.

Since you are already comfortable with grappling and fighting, you will not make the mistakes of untrained people or beginners, like turning their backs on the attacker as a means of shielding themselves. This is a natural response to a dangerous situation, but it puts you at a greater risk since you cannot see your opponent and anticipate their possible means of attack.

As someone trained in BJJ, you are more skilled and adept at protecting yourself and understanding your opponent's attacks, so you can easily set up measures to avoid them. You will also be more comfortable fighting and grappling with others, increasing your chance of winning the fight or escaping the situation unharmed.

Ideal for All People Regardless of Size

Knowing Brazilian Jiu-Jitsu will give you a fighting chance against an attacker or in a situation that requires you to defend yourself. The good thing about this form of martial arts is that it is perfect for everyone, regardless of size.

Even if you are small, you can still perform BJJ for self-defense. It will not pose the problems associated with smaller students of other martial arts training, such as their lighter bones and weight that may cause difficulty in inflicting damage on a bigger opponent. With Brazilian Jiu-Jitsu, even smaller individuals have a chance of defeating a bigger opponent.

Also, note that those with smaller physiques can generate limited force against their attackers or opponents. If you are bigger, expect that your hits will have more force because you have that added weight.

BJJ is such an incredible practice for self-defense as it teaches you how to choke and grapple larger and bigger individuals than you, negating the issue associated with the size.

Unlike Muay Thai, boxing, or any other form of martial arts that depends on athleticism, power, and speed, Brazilian Jiu-Jitsu focuses on technique. Smaller fighters can enforce a submission because of gaining confidence in their BJJ self-defense techniques.

A perfect example of the effectiveness of BJJ in dealing with bigger or larger opponents is Royce Gracie and his domination in UFC. In his fights, he was consistent in making his opponents submit regardless of their size. As far as ground technique is concerned, no other form of martial art compares to BJJ.

Helps You Stay in Control in a Fight

Brazilian Jiu-Jitsu is also perfect for self-defense as this form of martial art is highly effective in being able to control your opponent. You can use your BJJ skills to stop your attacker or opponent while ensuring that they do not get hurt or injured.

BJJ practice teaches you how to use leverage and frames to control the body weight of your opponent. Some positions, such as the knee-on-belly position, control an opponent on the ground.

You can also use a shoulder lock pose, which helps you to increase control over an attacker, especially if they are still untrained. If you are dealing with an attacker carrying a weapon, BJJ can't guarantee the highest level of protection, but it is still more advantageous compared to other forms of martial art, like Muay Thai.

Brazilian Jiu-Jitsu is more effective when dealing with situations involving a knife, as it teaches you to control your attacker. Positions like the Omoplata or shoulder lock will enable you to clearly observe your opponent's hand, giving you the edge over the opponent.

You will be at an advantage since you can clearly see what their next actions are. For instance, this gives you sufficient time to respond and stop the attack if they reach for the gun or knife.

Brazilian Jiu-Jitsu Self-Defense Techniques

When using Brazilian Jiu-Jitsu for self-defense, remember that strikes alone are not applicable, and it may be necessary to combine strikes with other BJJ tactics to be effective. However, most schools recommend starting your training without strikes, especially when executing stand-up grappling.

Only add strikes once you obtain a solid and stable grappling base. A second in time can make a significant difference, especially if the fight is fast-paced. That second could make you win or lose, so practice BJJ self-defense using your attacking knowledge.

Closed Guard

Guards in BJJ come in different formats, but for the purpose of self-defense, we will focus on the closed guard because this tactic is what grapplers currently use. It also carries several benefits when used in a self-defense situation.

The BJJ guard refers to how you use your legs when dealing with an adversary, like wrapping your legs around your adversary. You may do this lying on your back or keep the attacker or adversary away from you.

An appropriate use of the closed guard in a self-defense situation is to block punches.

Standing BJJ ArmBar

The standing armbar is an easy yet highly effective self-defense tactic you can learn from BJJ training, and it is also an effective combat submission technique. The standing armbar originated from Japanese Jiu-Jitsu.

It led to the seated version of the armbar that is often used in BJJ. The difference is that Japanese Jiu-Jitsu requires fighters to remain on their feet as there is a greater chance the opponents or fighters are using a weapon, like samurais.

Knee-On-Belly

This technique is vital if you want to be in control of your adversary or opponent. It is ideal in situations where you can grab the top position in a fight. In this position, use the knee-on-belly to move above your adversary easily. One example is when your adversary pulls a weapon, like a knife, from their boot or pocket while you control them through the knee-on-belly. You will have an easier time disengaging, moving away, or escaping from them.

Using a different move or position, such as the mount, may signify to your opponent that you are surrendering. It may also limit your movement, making it hard to disengage.

Cross-Face

This specific position requires you to be on top of your opponent or adversary to control them. Using your arm, go behind the head of your adversary or opponent. Place your shoulder to the side of your opponent's jawline. The pressure brought on by this position will give you control.

The correct execution of this technique and properly applied pressure from your shoulder will cause your opponent to look away and limit their movements. Since your opponent faces away from you, it is hard for them to execute any movements or techniques.

Side Control Escape

Many consider this technique the hardest position to escape from, and it comes in different variations. However, it would be best to learn the basic side control principles and disciplines so you can escape an attack.

Can You Use Brazilian Jiu-Jitsu When There Are Multiple Attackers?

As mentioned earlier, BJJ works perfectly in one-on-one confrontations. But the question is, will its self-defense techniques be effective when dealing with more than one attacker? The answer is no. This fighting system may be unsuitable to use against multiple opponents or on the battlefield.

The basic premise of self-defense is throwing an attacker or adversary to the floor. Speed is also vital in self-defense, and it is in this area where BJJ for self-defense may be at fault.

However, you can easily alter this if you spend time learning Judo throws instead of wrestling takedowns. Your goal would be to master throws capable of leaving your attacker on the ground while you are standing.

If possible, combine this with the other BJJ techniques and disciplines, and you can make the most of self-defense and reversal.

Where Can You Apply BJJ Self-Defense?

The effectiveness of BJJ as self-defense depends on the setting or location where the fight or altercation takes place. For instance, it would be difficult to use BJJ in a fight in a crowded bar; in this case, it would be much better to control your opponent from a standing position.

If the altercation occurs in an open space, such as a parking lot, and the attacker does not have a weapon, then the setting is suitable for BJJ self-defense skills.

You will have a better chance in an open space with takedowns since there are no barriers to control your attacker or assailant. The knee-on-belly is the best position to keep your assailant under control while sharpening your self-defense skills.

Chapter 6: Guards: Why Are They So Important to Know?

The Brazilian Jiu-Jitsu guard is one of the most useful and effective ground grappling positions to know. This position is characterized by a combatant with their back on the ground as they attempt to control their opponent with their legs.

The guard is a favorable position in mastering BJJ because you can attack your opponent using different chokeholds and joint locks from the bottom. On the other hand, the priority of your opponent on the top is to transition to a better and more dominant position. This is a process called passing the guard.

With the proven importance and undeniable benefits of this BJJ position, it is not surprising that it has several types. The type used will depend on your specific grips or points of control. Some Brazilian Jiu-Jitsu guards are ideal for use when you have an opponent in a standing position, and other guards work well when the opponent is kneeling.

When learning about BJJ guard positions, remember that some are perfect for grappling submissions but are harmful when used in MMA (mixed martial arts) tournaments. Other guard positions serve as a great escape or defense when dealing with the opponent's dominant positions.

Overall, the guard will always be a key component of Brazilian Jiu-Jitsu, considering its usefulness when fighting for an offensive position. In this chapter, you will learn more about the BJJ guard position, its different types, guard passing, sweep techniques, drills, and attacks. You will be able to make the most of this vital BJJ element after reading this chapter.

Closed Guard vs. Open Guards – The Differences

Two of the most basic and popular guard positions you will encounter are closed and open guards. Both are popular because they provide players with excellent tools, whether on the top or bottom.

The closed and open guards give you opportunities to sweep, control, and submit your opponent, establishing a strong and solid defensive and offensive grappling game.

Closed Guard

This is how to hold a strong closed guard

It is a basic type of guard that you will learn in your BJJ training. The closed guard is largely used by beginners and high-level competitors in BJJ. It is the founding guard and one of the first few positions you will learn as you begin your training in Brazilian Jiu-Jitsu.

Also called the full guard, the closed guard position occurs when you close your legs around the hips or waist of your opponent, and you must simultaneously grip your opponent's collar or sleeve.

The closed guard perfectly showcases the exact place where you can see the power and strength of guards in BJJ, specifically distance management, meaning you can be in complete control if you dictate the specific range that the grappling exchange takes place and have a free arm to use for attacks.

You also have to focus on successfully pulling through the vital aspects of the closed guard. These are discussed briefly.

- **Leg Position** - Wrap both your legs around the waist of your opponent, and interlock your ankles behind your opponent's back, securing the position. You may have to squeeze both your knees while bringing them simultaneously to your chest. It helps you to pull your opponent towards you, eliminating the space for their appropriate posture.

- **Grip** - Before performing the closed guard, think of the significance of grip placement because where you position your grip will give you the versatility to execute the move successfully.

  However, gripping from a closed guard position in most martial arts and self-defense situations, you will use the double sleeve/wrist grip. This grip allows you to control the arms of your opponent, keeping you safe from any form of attack.

- When you pair this grip with effective postural control, specifically with your legs, you will be in a dominant position to start your attack.

- **Goals** - Determine your goals when doing the guard, too. Like other guard types, your primary goal for the closed guard is to prevent your guard from being passed. Your goal is the only way to ensure that your guard is impenetrable, and that will help you start your attacks.

When making the attacks, it is beneficial to break your opponent's posture first. Note that you will be unable to attain much from an opponent who sits upright while implementing your chosen guard.

The good news is that effectively using your legs and the dual wrist grips help make your job easier. If they have broken posture, you can use sweeps, attacks, and back takes.

Open Guard

This is how to push for an open guard

The open guard differs from the closed guard because it does not require you to close your legs around your opponent's waist or chest. Use the open guard to transition from a half or weak full guard triggered by the opponent's movements.

There are several transitional positions, submissions, and sweeps when doing the BJJ open guard. For instance, you can transition to a butterfly, reverse De La Riva, De La Riva, and spider guards. It differs from the closed guard in a few aspects:

- **Leg Position** – Your legs have specific purposes in an open guard that stay the same no matter what the guard is. In the open guard, one leg will always serve as the hooking leg and is what you will attach to your opponent.

- You will use the other active leg based on what you want to execute, especially for guard retention, submissions, and sweeps. The exact leg positioning or placement will greatly depend on the type of open guard you intend to use.

- **Grips** – The open guard position allows a wide range of grip options. However, remember the underlying principle, which is always diagonal control. Preferably, you must grip a leg and the opposite side arm no matter which guard variation you use.

- **Goals** – An open guard position means that you will have to retain the position first before you can make an attack. Several open guard positions only provide a few attacks as they prioritize more on sweeps and off-balancing.

Other guard positions allow you to do chain sweeps and attacks and can force an opponent to be in a defensive position all the time.

Other BJJ Guard Types and Variations

Apart from the open and closed guards that are popular for BJJ beginners, there are also other types and variations to familiarize yourself with. These guards are useful o master every BJJ position and to win in a fight or attack.

High Guard

Trapping the opponent's shoulder in high guard

Also called the climbing or crooked guard. Maneuver your legs to climb up the opponent to trap one or both of their shoulders. Trapping the shoulders puts your opponent in danger because you can easily execute the armbar, sweep, and triangle attacks.

Compared to other types of guards, especially the rubber guard, the high guard requires only minimal flexibility. There are similarities, though, as they involve using both legs to keep the opponent's posture down. It is a fantastic BJJ guard, as your opponent will have a hard time striking you or passing your guard without providing you an opportunity for submission or sweep.

Deep Half Guard

The Deep Half Guard With triangled legs

In no gi, with one butterfly hook insterted under the opponent's lower leg

This guard position requires rolling beneath your opponent, so you can easily take their weight. Once you are in this position, use your legs to trap your opponent's legs while using both arms to grip around their hips. Swing your legs to take your opponent off balance. The deep half guard offers just a few submissions, but it is still a great position to sweep.

Rubber Guard

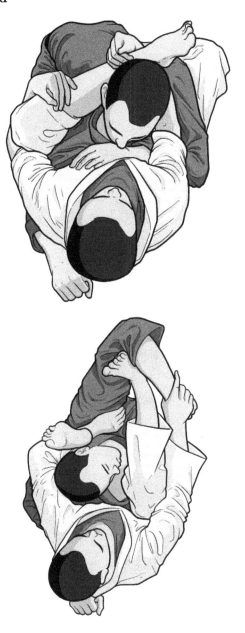

The rubber guard is challenging and tough to execute as it requires more flexibility. Execute this position if you are from a high or full guard. In Jiu-Jitsu, the rubber guard could be a variation of the high guard that requires you to use both feet and put them in a high position. This position helps you to control your opponent's neck and ensures that his head stays down. The result is perfect control of your opponent, who will be in a poor BJJ posture.

Spider Guard

The Spider Guard being used against a kneeling opponent (both feet on biceps)

Against a standing opponent, one foot on biceps and the other on the hip

Against a standing opponent using one foot on the bicep and one leg wrapped around the arm

The spider guard is a tough BJJ position that you can use to gain excellent control of your distance in the kneeling or standing opponent. This position can contribute to putting your opponent off balance, giving you opportunities for a few submissions or sweeps, including the arm bar and triangle chokes.

You can also use the spider guard to transition to other BJJ guards, such as the De La Riva. You can execute it as an open guard by gripping the sleeves or wrists of your opponent, and using one foot to control their arms, too.

In most cases, you only have to put one foot against their biceps; otherwise, your leg is at risk of spiraling near their elbow, and your toes are hiding beneath their upper arm.

Butterfly Guard

The Butterfly Guard an underhook and a belt grip

Using a pant leg and lapel cross grip

The Butterfly Guard in no gi using a bearhug grip. Occasionally used in MMA, since it is
difficult for the opponent to generate a lot of force in his strikes.

A very difficult position from which to play the Butterfly Guard (referred to as the TK Guard by early UFC commentators.

This dynamic butterfly guard position features several options for sweeps and can be used in no-Gi and Gi grappling. To execute this guard, first, familiarize yourself with the sitting position and how to remain active when trying to get your opponent off-balance.

Many fighters in Brazilian Jiu-Jitsu use this position to initialize leg lock submissions. Some use this position to transition to half guard, single leg X guard, and X guard positions.

Knee Shield or Z-Guard

The Z Guard with the bottom leg hooking and the top knee pushing at the hip

The same position with the top knee pushing in the chest / shoulder area

You can execute this specific guard from the standard half-guard position. Raise one knee to take the weight off your opponent. It creates a skeletal frame, ensuring that you will not be crushed by your opponent when threatened with submissions and sweeps. To defend a submission, attack the far arm, and to enact the sweeps, get the nearside under hook and simultaneously threaten the back.

Octopus Guard

The Octopus Guard in no-gi

In most cases, you get an opening for the octopus guard position when your opponent executes a hip switch after being in a knee shield position. Another way to do the octopus guard is to move your far shoulder behind your opponent's.

Use this specific position to sweep into the mount or reach the back. Otherwise referred to as the reverse half guard, the octopus guard also requires you to base or depend on your elbow to get into the position.

Koala Guard

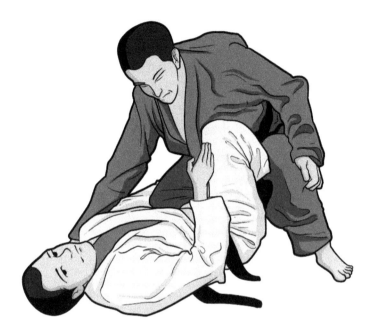

Koala Guard

You can do the koala guard position as you get into a sitting position against a standing opponent. Latch onto your opponent's leg, similar to how a koala does, while hugging them, leading to a tighter connection. The koala guard is frequently used to transition to other guard positions, and it is also useful whenever you need to attack leg locks, like foot locks, Achilles' locks, and knee bars.

Collar Sleeve Guard

Collar Sleeve Guard

To get into this guard position, use one of your hands to grab your opponent's sleeve, the other hand to grab the collar, and put your leg on the sleeve's bicep that is in your grip.

Place your other leg on your opponent's hip. Alternatively, you can wrap this leg into a hook. Like other sleeve guards, your goal when executing the collar sleeve guard is pushing and pulling your opponent off-balance. You can effectively hit different sweeps and prompt a submission, which is usually the triangle.

Quarter Guard

Quarter Guard

This position is between a mount defense and the half guard. In most cases, the quarter guard provides little for attacks, so it is mainly used as a retention position to stop you from passing your guard.

Most fighters are not fond of the quarter guard because it is categorized as an inferior position. This position depends on keeping the foot of the opponent trapped rather than their knee. Despite that, it is still useful for sweeps when your opponent makes a mistake.

What Is Guard Retention?

Now that you know some of the most useful guards, it is time to understand how you can retain this position. As a BJJ beginner, besides mastering different guard positions, you also have to learn how to retain them.

The goal of mastering guard retention is to avoid being overcome by the opponent's guard passes without getting the chance to retain the position. Act immediately whenever you sense that your opponent is about to pass your guard.

Of course, the first step in handling this dilemma is to remain calm. Facing your opponent is also necessary. Remember that for you to pass the guard, your opponent has to come to your side and get into side control. So, you want to continue rotating your body to ensure that you're facing your opponent all the time.

In doing so, they will be unable to get to the pose that will prompt you to pass the guard. The primary guard retention principle you must always remember is to *face your attacker or opponent.*

Keeping the Head under Control

Do not worry if your opponent is already halfway in his attempt to make you pass your guard, as it is still possible to save and restore your position. The best way to handle this situation is to control your opponent's head by using both hands.

It will prevent your opponent from moving efficiently and prioritizing dealing with your hands, giving you sufficient time to move your body away. Use this time to reset your main position, which is also essential for effective guard retention.

Proper Knee Positioning

Proper knee positioning is also crucial in guard retention. The goal is to ensure that your knees continue to stay together as much as possible, but it does not necessarily mean keeping your knees closed without putting any space in between. The best position for your knees is to keep them very close to your chest. Your opponent would have a hard time making you pass your guard if you managed to keep your knees close to your chest successfully.

However, you must also learn how to pull away from your legs to create an opening for your side-control entry. Guard retention is possible if you make sure that your opponent stays close to you.

Chapter 7: The Art of Takedown

Takedowns are vital to Brazilian Jiu-Jitsu, so all participants must know how to perform them regardless of belts, expertise, and skill levels. In BJJ competitions, the fight starts in a natural standing position, but you will earn valuable points if you land a good takedown. The takedown also defines how the fight will end.

What is even better about having a good drop is that it provides you with an excellent ground position, like side-control and mount positions. It even gives you the opportunity to take the back of your opponent.

Why Learning the Art of Takedown Is Important for BJJ

When grasping the importance of takedowns in BJJ, it is crucial to understand the roots of this form of martial art – one of which is self-defense and extremely significant. Takedowns offer an opportunity for a quick escape when you need to defend yourself or execute your ground fighting skills.

Mastering good takedowns is crucial as it provides you with great defense skills, especially if the situation involves more than one attacker. Almost everyone believes that in street fights, the ground is probably the least favored area.

Yes, your training in Brazilian Jiu-Jitsu has offered you a strong physical edge whenever you get into the ground, but it would be best to avoid it if you are in danger. Your goal would be a quick escape, and your knowledge of takedowns will enable you to achieve that.

Takedowns are also vital in rules that penalize guard pulling and indicate whether you should start the match from a position on top. Moreover, the takedown will serve as a surprise for an attacker or your opponent in competitions.

Never underestimate the importance of takedowns not only in BJJ competitions but also when you are faced with dangerous situations.

Takedown Fundamentals

All combat sports and martial arts, like Brazilian Jiu-Jitsu, consider the ability to take someone down as a vital aspect. Your takedown skill will be valuable self-defense during street fights. With a successful throw or takedown, you weaken your attacker or opponent's position, putting them in a difficult and vulnerable spot to your advantage.

It's imperative first to learn the fundamentals of takedowns so you can successfully pull them off. This section gives the concepts, tips, and exercises to improve your takedowns.

Targeting the Weak Plane

The weak plane is a fundamental aspect of takedown that BJJ beginners must learn and understand. The weak plane refers to the point that forms a triangle using the line you visualize when you connect your two feet. In this line, you will find your center of gravity.

For instance, if an attacker or opponent stands square with their feet parallel on the ground, their weak plane is most likely directly backward or forward. Remember that the weak plane changes constantly, but it will not disappear.

Once you improve your proficiency in performing takedowns, it will be easier for you to automatically feel the exact spot of your opponent's weak plane. You can use it to determine the perfect direction to do the takedown in just a single glance.

Off-Balance Your Opponent

When executing takedowns, learning how to off-balance your attacker or opponent is extremely important; it is extremely difficult to take down your opponent if they have perfect balance. Also called *kuzushi* in Judo, you can off-balance your opponent through drags and snap downs.

You can also do it by pulling their Gi, causing them to step off-balance. The act of off-balancing your opponent works along with targeting the weak plane, and the reason is that you can use this technique to expose the weak plane of your opponent.

The goal is to force your opponent to step in a particular direction allowing easier access to their weak plane. It also helps expose the leg of your opponent, promoting further ease in executing the takedowns.

Other Fundamental Strategies and Concepts

Every grappling style has its own fundamental concept, which improves its level of effectiveness. The following are among the key and fundamental strategies and concepts that will improve your takedown abilities even further:

Takedown Roadmap

It is necessary to improve your ability to chain together the sequences for takedowns and combine them with various clenching setups. In other words, you must build a roadmap with the specific techniques worthwhile to pair up or combine.

Creating a roadmap will also help you with specific clinching positions guaranteed to work for you, depending on your opponent's reaction. Roadmaps contribute to building a strong and solid foundation for moving from all possible takedowns and setups.

Head Position Fighting and Manipulation

Make sure that you also know how to fight for and manipulate the head position of your opponent using your forehead. This action will impede their vision and keep them off balance. Remember, when grappling, the head serves as the fifth limb. You can consider yourself an excellent grappler if you know how to push your opponent by using your head.

Grab and Go

When fighting a larger opponent who is most likely superior in strength, focus on using setup movements allowing you to grab them quickly and disrupt their posture or balance right away. While they are recovering, make openings to use for your preferred takedowns.

Train yourself to perform the movements rapidly, and your opponent will not be able to hold or grab you. If you fail during your first attempt, disengage. Some examples of grab-and-go moves are snap downs and arm drags.

Let Your Opponents Guess Your Next Moves

The repeated use of similar technique combinations and moves is not good BJJ, as your opponent will have an easier time predicting and countering your movements. Make use of your takedown roadmap to avoid this. Ensure that the roadmap is extensive enough to eliminate predictability in your fights. Change your takedown combinations and positional setups frequently and keep your opponent guessing all the time.

Move Opponents to Your Preferred Positions

During your fights, ensure that your tactics will encourage your opponent to move into the position you intended. For example, if you are doing the single leg takedown while engaging in a clinch, move your hands so that they slide forward to gain double bicep control.

If the arm on the side of your lead leg side is pulled, take advantage of your footwork and force your opponent to move with your body instead of utilizing the strength of your arms.

Expect your opponent to step forward to maintain their balance. This step will most likely be on the pulled arm's side, resulting in their lead leg matching yours. It is the perfect time to shoot into a single leg.

Essential Takedowns That BJJ Beginners Must Know

To start mastering the art of takedowns, here are the essential ones for BJJ beginners:

Double Leg

A double-leg takedown is a vital takedown technique that has many BJJ applications. It is challenging to make a list of beginner takedowns without including the double leg. It is the most commonly used takedown in martial arts because the technique is simple and easy to understand.

To execute the double leg takedown successfully, you must first change levels, meaning bringing your head down to the belt-line of your opponent and performing the penetration step. You must grab the legs of your opponent and then drive through.

Practice this technique often, and you will immediately notice an improvement in catching your attackers or opponents off-guard, catching them with this technique when they least expect it. Note that while you can execute the double leg explosively, it is often unnecessary.

It would be much better to slowly start when practicing and build gradually to provide your partner with enough time to break the fall.

Ankle Pick

This takedown is probably the most effective technique adapted by BJJ. The relative simplicity of the ankle pick technique is why it is one of the first taught in BJJ and other martial arts.

To perform the ankle pick takedown, push your opponent's head over one of their legs, immobilizing the leg as it will bear excess weight. While the leg cannot move, complete this takedown technique by stepping in; this is necessary for blocking the target foot before you reach down and grab the ankle.

At this point, raise the opponent's foot leading to the takedown or fall of your opponent. As you may have observed, this technique is not like other takedowns that involve high-amplitude slams and throws. You just have to pluck one foot of your opponent from beneath him, and he will fall safely to the mat.

One advantage of the ankle pick takedown is that the penalty for failure is very low. Also, unlike what is usually involved in conventional wrestling, it is unnecessary to enter beneath your opponent when executing the ankle pick, eliminating the possibility of getting crushed beneath your opponent's weight.

Another reason to train for the ankle pick takedown is that it teaches grapplers to prioritize their takedown strategies during live competitions and rounds without frustration. It is also an incredible technique to learn if you're uncomfortable with your game when in a standing position.

Single Leg Takedown

As a vital technique in wrestling, single-leg takedown is also useful in Brazilian Jiu-Jitsu. This technique is more strength-dependent compared to other takedowns. In Brazilian Jiu-Jitsu, particularly the no-Gi, several sweeps result in single-leg takedowns, so you must learn how to finish a single leg when involved in no-Gi grappling.

Performing the single-leg takedown, first change levels, then hook your left arm around your opponent's right knee while pivoting to your left leg. Lift your opponent's leg from the ground while you connect your hands and maintain closed elbows. Ensure that the topmost part of your head drives to the chest of your opponent, too. Pinch their leg between yours.

Finish this technique with a double-leg takedown. Using your right hand, grab the knee of your opponent's base leg; this will encourage the execution of the double leg. You may also end it up with a foot sweep - sweep out their base leg with one of your feet.

High Crotch

The high crotch is a cross from the single and the double leg takedowns. The high crotch does not need the athleticism required by the double leg. However, you must have a more technical aptitude than the single leg when executing this takedown.

Similar to the single leg takedown, shoot for the lead leg when executing the high crotch. However, your head must be at the outside of the attacker or opponent rather than inside.

Collar Drag

The collar drag is a common takedown that is only applicable in Brazilian Jiu-Jitsu. It is a popular guard sweep you can also execute when standing and is very easy to learn, which is why it forms part of the arsenal of most BJJ participants.

The collar drag is easy to learn as it does not require you to get under your opponent's center of gravity, and it is also not necessary to do a lot of off-balancing. Moreover, the collar drag's motion is similar to pulling a half guard.

To execute the collar drag, give your opponent a cross collar grip using your right hand and let your left foot step outside of your opponent's right foot. Slide one leg between the legs of your opponent and drop your right hip to the floor.

Visualize pulling the half guard. While sliding the right hip and leg, yank the collar of your opponent to the ground. Your knees must end the takedown and drive into your attacker or opponent if needed.

Chapter 8: The Art of Submissions

The art of submission in Brazilian Jiu-Jitsu, also recognized as the Gentle Art, serves as your pinnacle of success when mastering this martial art. Note all BJJ participants will always go after a submission despite the fact that many BJJ tournaments and matches end on points.

As a beginner, you may get overwhelmed with the numerous submissions you have to learn, monitor, and master. Well, don't panic. You only need to learn the basic categories of submissions in BJJ to grasp the fundamental principles and have an easier time submitting your opponent.

How to Make Every BJJ Submission Work

There are many BJJ submissions, so remembering each of them as single tactics and techniques may be difficult. However, once you determine the specific reasons for submissions and familiarize yourself with the categorization system, you can fully understand each and master them easily. Another crucial point is that those specific aspects of ending submissions are considered universal for each terminal Brazilian Jiu-Jitsu move; thus, positioning is an important factor and concept. As you hunt for submissions, positioning most of your body against a single part of your opponent's body is necessary. Using your strong body parts, you will have an easier time attacking your opponent's weaker parts.

Grips are also among the most vital aspects of BJJ submission because you can either make or break your intended submission attempts. Grips contribute a lot to building tension in the specific body parts you intend to attack. You can also use the proper grips to apply torsion to introduce a twisting motion in each submission.

These are a few mechanical principles that serve as the major elements of performing Jiu-Jitsu submissions. However, remind yourself that various submissions also operate using various fundamentals, meaning that you can only monitor all these submissions if you categorize them into a sensible system.

Effective Brazilian Jiu-Jitsu Submission Techniques

This section also gives you an idea of how you can organize the submissions to easily remember them.

Moreover, you will learn how to get several taps. To understand various submissions easily, divide them based on their primary categories, with each category having specific sub-categories regarding tactics and techniques.

Strangles (Chokes)

Chokes or strangles are straightforward and easily understandable, and it involves wrapping something around an opponent's neck and tightening it. There are four strangle techniques to obtain BJJ submissions – three can be used as finishing strangles.

- Air chokes by closing the trachea
- Chest compressions by preventing chest expansion through pressure
- Blood chokes by compressing carotid arteries on both sides of your opponent's neck

It is also possible to do the neck crank, even though this move falls under the spinal locks category. When performing chokes, an important principle to remember is to make sure you plug the hole.

You can't expect any choke to work if space is still left around the opponent's neck. By putting every structural element together, you must plug the hole and increase the chance of a successful choke.

Also, it is crucial to exercise patience when waiting for the choke to take hold. Once you are sure that the choke is set, count to 20, readjust if the opponent still does not tap out, and use a squeeze or do the choke again.

Submissions that fall under the choke or strangle category are discussed next.

Rear-Naked Choke

This vital Brazilian Jiu-Jitsu submission is a must for beginners to learn. The rear-naked choke often operates from back control, especially when your arms surround your opponent's neck. You can reinforce this move by placing the remaining arm in a configuration that resembles figure 4.

Let your elbows stick to your chest and sides. Do this while you are squeezing to ensure that you can plug the hole, ensuring that you obtain adequate torsion and tension, too. This choke is legal in every BJJ belt and is applicable with or without Gi.

Guillotine Choke

Guillotine Choke

Unlike the rear-naked choke, the guillotine choke refers to a submission from the front, frequently from the guard, among other positions. To execute this choke perfectly, ensure that your opponent's head gets under your armpit. Follow this up with the vital chin strap grip.

Completing the guillotine choke depends significantly on the exact variation you decide to use. Also, the choke may work as an air or blood choke since there is an element of chest compression in each version.

The guillotine choke produces favorable results whether you use a Gi or not. You can also do it from the guard, standing, half-guard, and mount positions. Also, it has several variations, including the high elbow, power guillotine, ten-finger, low elbow, and arm-in.

Triangle Choke

Triangle Choke

As a vital grappling submission, the triangle choke involves using your opponent's legs and his arm. This specific choke variation originated from Judo, but it is a famous BJJ submission nowadays as it delivers a good performance regardless of the position and with or without a Gi.

You can initiate the triangle choke submission from a closed guard. However, it is versatile to initiate it from other moves, like open guards, back control, half guard, mount, and standing.

Grapefruit or Helio Gracie Choke

Grapefruit or Helio Gracie Choke

Many BJJ practitioners are fond of this BJJ submission as it provides a simple method of choking an opponent out. It's a traditional choke you can do from a mount, positioning the knuckles on both sides of your opponent's neck.

Clench your fists when doing this, and it also helps to put your elbows on the ground to access an excellent position that allows your knuckles to put direct pressure on the artery. It is a quick submission that is effective and painful.

Bow and Arrow Choke

Bow and Arrow Choke

This specific choke is similar to a collar choke initiated from the back control. You can perform it by grabbing your opponent's leg and lapel while keeping the movement in their legs under control.

The name of this submission is derived from the configured two bodies when the choke is executed. You may also initiate the bow and arrow choke from the closed guard, side control, and turtle.

Arm and Shoulder Locks

Another BJJ submission category to familiarize yourself with is the arm and shoulder lock. Most of the submissions that fall in this category involve attacking the arm's joints, including the shoulders, wrist, and elbow, and it is the most commonly used submission today.

Although the arm lock is in various sub-categories, it will greatly depend on whether the target arm is bent or straight aside from attacking the joint. The primary principle that governs all arm locks is the importance of controlling two of the neighboring joints on both sides of your opponent.

Armbar

Armbar

The armbar involves the use of a straight arm while targeting the joints of the elbow. Once you have completed the top or bottom grapple, use your hips to press on your opponent's elbow forcing your opponent to bend in an unwanted and wrong direction.

Your hips and legs have complete control over your opponent's shoulder joints, and your torso and arms also affect their wrist. This specific submission is often set from the guard or mount. However, almost every position provides an armbar entry. This submission is legal for everyone and tends to work well whether you wear a Gi or not.

Straight Armlock

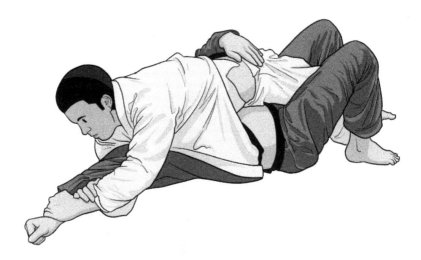

Straight Armlock

This specific submission typically starts from either the bottom or top. If you do it from the guard, it will be called the inverted armlock. The ultimate goal is to use your arms to add pressure on the elbow instead of the hips. Your legs are also expected to control the joint of your opponent's shoulders. Use your head to block the wrist, and use your shoulder to trap the arm.

Kimura

Kimura

This submission falls under the bent armlocks category, which often targets the opponent's shoulder joints. It is a popular form of Jiu-Jitsu submission that many fighters use. Using the figure 4 grip configuration, target your opponent's wrist.

It means that you will control the elbow using leverage and your legs to care for the neck. The Kimura involves a twisting motion with the arms and torso, but the hold can break if not done effectively.

Americana

Americana

The Americana submission serves as a Kimura while also having a bent arm in an opposite direction. This form of submission is exclusive to fighters in top positions, especially if you consider the arm's direction. The Americana will be effective once you get a figure-4 grip on the opponent's wrist.

Make sure to use your elbow to block your opponent's neck allowing the grip to handle the opponent's elbow. Drag the palms back across the mat towards your opponent's hip.

The Americana is possible from the mount, top half guard, and side control. There are no strict restrictions regarding who can make this submission, and the Americana can be used with many other armlocks.

Squirrel Lock

Many consider the squirrel lock as the sneakiest of all armlock submissions in Brazilian Jiu-Jitsu. You can get a tap from this move by using your legs. However, it is quite different as the bottom side control makes it preferable, and the entire submission is very unexpected.

The entire setup needs tinkering and training. However, essentially, you are executing a Kimura since you use your legs to entangle the opponent's far arm and finish from the bottom. You may also wrap up the entire process by rolling over on top.

Neck Crank

Neck Crank

The neck crank falls under the spinal lock category and is a simple form of submission. It is executed by bending your opponent's neck in a specific direction that adds pressure to their spine. This fairly dangerous move may cause a lot of pain, so you have to be extra careful.

The neck crank has different variations – among which are the following:

- **Can Opener** – This is a submission move that has earned a bad reputation. The can opener is executed from the guard's inside. Your goal is to cusp your opponent's head using both hands, similar to the Thai clinch. Bend the neck forward, adding extra pressure by using your hips.

- **From the Mount** – If you initiate the neck crank from the mount, you will realize how easy and simple it is to execute. The process is quite intuitive for many, as it allows you to execute a rare naked choke initiated from the mount.

  o   An arm goes around your opponent's head, and while setting the grip, your palm ends on your opponent's forehead. It may involve nasty pressure as you have to let your forearm press on the spine directly.

- **From the Back** – You can also do the neck crank from the back control. When you start from the back, there are plenty of BJJ submissions you can do. Ensure that the forearm goes across the jaw, allowing the opponent's head to turn to one side, and finish by keeping your arms locked in a palm-to-palm grip, preventing pulling.

Hip Lock

Hip Lock

The hip lock is also another category of Brazilian Jiu-Jitsu submissions with a couple of variations.

- **Banana Split** – This specific hip lock you can initiate if you are in a turtle position. Trap one leg of your opponent using your legs and arms to trap the other leg and extend away from their legs, contributing to a painful and uncomfortable hip lock.

- **Electric Chair** – This submission form is a groin stretch and a sweep that you can initiate from a half-guard and lockdown position. You can execute this submission if you establish a lockdown. Use your hands to force your opponent off-balance, then grab their leg.

Finish this by keeping the leg on your shoulder. This form of submission will not always work on versatile opponents, meaning there is also a chance to get to your opponent's knees as they maintain the grips for the guard pass initiation.

Foot Lock

The foot lock submission comes in a wide range of variations. The ones you use in BJJ will always include the following.

Straight Ankle Lock

This submission targets the joints in your ankle and your Achilles tendon. Do this as you immobilize your opponent's leg using both your legs and wrap your arm around your opponent's foot.

Hyperextend the foot away and down from the leg; it is possible if you arch the back. This versatile submission is accessible from numerous positions, like the half guard, back control, and leg drag pass.

Kneebar

The kneebar submission efficiently works when done in a specific position. Your goal when doing the kneebar is to sit on your opponent's hips and hug their legs before falling to your side.

This position gives adequate space to triangle your legs and focus on getting into a figure-4 grip on the leg. If performed correctly, it is possible to break your opponent's knee. To execute the break, extend your hips, and twist your shoulders to the ceiling. Note that only Black and Brown Belt fighters are permitted to do the kneebar.

Chapter 9: Combining What You Have Learned: More Advanced Techniques

After learning the basic techniques designed for beginners in Brazilian Jiu-Jitsu, it is time to move on to more advanced techniques, probably to intermediate. When you can master the basic BJJ techniques and proficiently use them in a match, it is time to think about combinations.

One straightforward attack may not be enough, especially when dealing with an expert and experienced opponent. Expert and skilled opponents will immediately detect your intentions before you even get the chance to make a move and put up a defense.

Intermediate and advanced belts are required to create attacks that use various tactical and technical combinations. The action-reaction principle discussed in a previous chapter is vital in attaining success with attack combinations. When you attempt to execute your primary or first attack, your opponent will put up a defense, exposing them to your second attack.

Importance of Learning Combinations

The ultimate secret to becoming a well-rounded fighter in Brazilian Jiu-Jitsu and all martial arts is to learn combinations. Your knowledge of strikes and throw combinations can separate a beginner from a skilled and experienced BJJ fighter.

Newbies in martial arts, especially in Brazilian Jiu-Jitsu, have yet to learn how to throw combinations with any form of structure and fluency. Each tactic and move is still new, making it hard for them to combine multiple tactics while learning and understanding the basics. However, as soon as you gain more experience, you can move to a more advanced level that teaches these combinations.

The ability to do combinations is crucial in all BJJ competitions and training. If you cannot perform any combination, it will be extremely difficult for you to beat a skilled and experienced opponent because skilled fighters will defend themselves from a single strike or takedown you throw.

Integrating feints, tricks, and follow-ups to your attacks, strokes, or throws, can change the intensity of a fight. No matter how experienced and defensive a fighter is, they will still be overwhelmed if you combine various takedowns and punches. An attempt to set up a defense for one attack may lead to the opening of a counterattack.

If you have only learned to throw singular jabs, it will be impossible to hit an experienced striker's head. Your moves will be predictable to your opponent.

A single attack executed alone is useless when used against an experienced opponent and will only be effective when fighting an untrained and inexperienced opponent.

Using Combinations in BJJ

As you have already discovered, Brazilian Jiu-Jitsu is a ground-fighting martial art. This martial art aims to sweep your opponent and force them to submit. It becomes part of the fighter's toolkit when on the floor.

Similar to Judo, Brazilian Jiu-Jitsu also concentrates on the weight distribution of you and your opponent. Any time your opponent positions their arm or leg incorrectly, you can attack them and use your opponent's incorrect position to make them lie on their backs on the mat.

In BJJ, combinations are used similarly to Judo. For instance, you can chain together several attacks to catch your adversary or opponent off-guard and obtain complete control of their back.

Some BJJ skilled fighters can switch from an armbar and a rear-naked choke, or vice versa, ensuring that their opponents cannot guess what attack will come next.

By chaining many attacks together, your opponent will have a hard time finding answers and defenses, and it will be challenging for them to put up a defense that would result in a submission.

So, what are the combinations you can use to become a more well-rounded and skilled BJJ fighter? These combos are among the best answers:

Chaining Combinations

This specific combo can move and transition through several different attacks and deal with various submission escapes and defenses. Start this combination from the knee-on-stomach position, then establish a strong and stable spinning armbar.

Hug the arm of your opponent tightly, ensuring that it is held close to your body, and plant your foot close to the opponent's shoulder. Your opponent might try to come out on top during the transition, so it's important to remain tight.

Turn your body over to position yourself correctly for your next attack, the kimura that you will start from the bottom. Use this technique to flip your opponent over so they will be in an armbar position.

While straightening the arm, your opponent may turn up their thumb in a runaway or hitchhiker to break free from the armbar. Essentially, they will be running around in circles as they try to escape successfully. Allow your opponent to continue while you transition to the Omoplata as you alter your angle and kick your leg through.

Your opponent might posture up, preparing to defend themselves from the Omoplata, switch to the triangle. The goal of this technique is that as soon as you feel you're losing your attacked submission, you should switch to a new submission.

To ensure that you get excellent results from this combo, get a feel of your opponent as they escape your submission. Let them have slight chances for an escape as they serve as your opening for another attack. You will learn the things that work and what doesn't.

Combo That Lets Your Lower Body Flow

This is a relatively short combo designed for the flow drill but can give highly favorable results. It is a great combination to use your opponent does more work than you as they roll. Begin by setting up for the execution of the inverted heel hook. As soon as you start torquing the heel of your opponent, retain your grip as they try circling to escape.

You may be inclined to follow your opponent at this point, which is not a poor tactic if you are one hundred percent sure you can finish the initial attack. However, if they get even just half a step ahead, it would be best to let them escape while you determine your next move.

While they are circling, resist the urge to alter your hip's position, except when you do the kneebar finish. If you have already performed the kneebar, let your partner continue circling or rotating beyond the kneebar. It will serve as your starting point for the simple switch to the 50/50 position that you can use to finish the game with a heel hook.

Guard Passing and Submission Attack Combo

This specific tactic provides you with a means of combining a guard pass or positional advance with a submission. What is great about this combo is that it is designed to bring your game to a whole new level because it's hard to defend a submission attack and guard pass simultaneously.

Your opponent may even have a hard time defending themselves as you perform these moves one after another. As soon as they addressed the first attack, you have already moved into another attack, making it challenging for them to keep up.

For this specific technique, begin by doing a knee-cut guard pass. The key to quickly finishing the pass is to use the under hook often. However, if your opponent still triumphs during the under hook fight, you can back step into a solid kneebar attack.

Wait for your opponent to triangle their legs to defend themselves from the kneebar, then slide to finish the fight with a straight ankle lock submission.

Guard to Triangle Choke

Guard to Triangle Choke

If you are searching for a trendy technique, a triangle choke from any form of the guard is the most viable move. The triangle choke is extremely popular in BJJ as every fighter seems to be using it, from the white to the black belts. The triangle choke is an indispensable technique in MMA and other global competitions for Gi and no-Gi.

To perform this combination, attack your opponent using both your legs and from the bottom. This specific technique is effective, especially if your opponent is larger than you. In this case, you may have a hard time reversing positions and getting yourself on top.

Start from any type of guard and set up the triangle choke differently, but be very sure that you are familiar with the mechanisms of the guard you choose. You must study various ways to exact the guard to perfection.

Also, be careful not to use the triangle choke to attack once your opponent is in a good position and posture. Your chances of winning will drop since an excellent posture is the most reliable position for defense with the triangle choke.

Making the Most Out of BJJ Combinations

Experts and legends in BJJ all agree on how important it is to use sequences and combinations for a participant to experience exponential growth. As soon as you move to the intermediate level and learn the basics look for sequences or tactics that you can proficiently and comfortably execute. Practice them with your training partner regularly.

It is also crucial to find dynamic partners, specifically those that will not defend your attempts for submission but move enough to challenge you to master your combinations. The advantage of this is that it directs you towards a new level of progress.

You must adapt to the sequences and combinations you created based on the effort and movements exerted and executed by your training partner. You will be forced to understand when and how to use other tactics when necessary; this is the key to reinforcing and strengthening your already expanding skillset in Brazilian Jiu-Jitsu.

Chapter 10: Weight Pressure and Energy Control

Pressure is another important aspect and concept to master in Brazilian Jiu-Jitsu. Even during the first stages of your beginner training in BJJ, you will already know that pressure can significantly improve your grappling skills.

Applying pressure in a BJJ practice or fight helps hold the other person down for an extended period, leading to setting up a submission. It is also necessary to apply pressure whenever you need to pass the guard or execute certain moves and positions. Pressure is also required to improve the effectiveness of your submissions from the top.

Types of Pressure in Brazilian Jiu-Jitsu

In Brazilian Jiu-Jitsu, the term "pressure" means more than merely the concept of weight or how heavy an opponent is. In most cases, it revolves around controlled points and the specific manner you can hold these points.

Pressure also enables you to retain control when executing major positions, including mount, back mount, and side control. This pressure comes in three forms.

Weight Distribution

An area in BJJ you must focus on is weight distribution, a vital element or concept of BJJ that's also classified as pressure. Unlike speed and strength that diminishes as you age, your skills in using your weight to your best advantage do not.

It means you must use your weight properly to expend less energy while your opponent is at risk of exerting more. The correct use of your weight will force an opponent in a lower belt to become fatigued faster. On the other hand, if you are fighting against a higher belt, you can use your weight to frustrate them.

Note that when dealing with those with higher belts, you will need more time mastering how to use your weight to your best advantage, but you will eventually grasp it with constant practice.

For example, when you take the top position, quickly eliminate the points of contact your opponent has with the ground. These points of contact include the shoulders, the back of your opponent's head, and elbows.

It may force your opponent to handle your weight on the soft midsection, and pressure applied to this area can greatly affect their breathing. Also, to ensure that you use the weight distribution to your advantage, take note of the following:

- **Weight on Top** - Back mount, side control, guard passing, mount
- **Weight on the Bottom** - Closed guard. It is highly recommended to consistently use both your legs' weight on your opponent's back while ensuring that there are assisting angles.
- **Angling Weight** - A certain angle to your opponent causes you to become heavier because of the discomfort.
- **Shifting Weight** - Lifting hips, dropping hips, rotating

One sign that you are correctly distributing your weight is when there is only minimal holding and squeezing, meaning that you expend minimal energy while your opponent exerts more.

Another way to improve using your weight is to lessen your movement and use more gravity. Your opponent will feel like they are beneath a heavy wet blanket or drowning in cement.

It is crucial to concentrate on your breathing when defending your weight. Aside from that, focus on getting better postural alignments by ensuring that your knees remain beneath your waistline. It helps prevent your weight from crushing a rib or your leg from rotating inward, injuring the knee ligaments.

Pain Compliance Pressure

Pain compliance pressure is often found in catch wrestling, but many also use it in Jiu-Jitsu and regular grappling. It is used as a means to force rapid openings and reactions to achieve submission.

What's great about using the pain compliance pressure is that it can elicit sharp and quick responses from your opponents. Your opponent will respond by panicking, jumping, or even flinching, and these are the responses you are hoping to get from applying this pressure.

However, the pain compliance pressure will not be effective when used against an opponent holding a higher belt or rank because most high-ranked and advanced fighters will have already mastered feeling comfortable in discomfort.

Still, you can enjoy using pain compliance pressure in the following techniques with the right opponent.

- **Sawing** – This technique requires using the elbow to apply pressure to your opponent's pressure points. It could be the front deltoid or the jaw.

- **Shoulder Pressure** – Use the shoulder pressure starting from the side control, and crush your opponent's jaw or execute a choke resulting in a fast response from your opponent.

- **Muffler** – This technique requires restricting the airway. It falls under pain compliance pressure as it can elicit a pain reaction from the opponent.

- **Knee to Belly or Neck** – This technique also belongs to the weight distribution pressure. The knee applies pressure to the opponent's neck or stomach, causing their sharp reactions.

Before using pain compliance pressure, remember that you can't expect it to work with advanced BJJ fighters, so you must prepare before using these pressure tactics. You will become proficient in using pain compliance pressure tactics for fights, tournaments, and self-defense effectively through regular practice.

Panic Pressure

The last type of pressure that you can use in Brazilian Jiu-Jitsu is panic pressure. You will most likely feel this panic pressure if you are in the early stages of your BJJ training. Your panic may be due to worrying that you will land in bad positions all the time, causing you not to breathe properly or think clearly. Worse, you will always be thinking that you are at risk of submission.

However, after much practice and your acquisition of more knowledge and skills, everything becomes less stressful. You will learn to use the panicky feeling to deal with your opponent.

When you advance to a higher level, you can induce panic in a lower belt to win by applying panic pressure when you are in a dominant position. Your goal is to control your opponent so they feel there is no point of escape.

You can start this tactic with position control – having positional control and dominance, preventing any possible means of escape. If your intended submissions are not yet available and your opponent is still full of energy and vitality, stop their means of escape by focusing more on countering their moves. They will become frustrated to the point of panic.

If you suspect your opponent is at this point, do some sub-attempts. Control the position, and threaten them with their leg, neck, or arm to elicit a panic or frustration response. Your opponent will feel they are backed into a corner with no other choice but to submit

Energy Management and Its Importance in BJJ

Out of the many principles that govern Brazilian Jiu-Jitsu, energy management has its level of importance. Many BJJ participants overlook energy management and fail to see its importance in winning fights. Imagine what will happen to you during a fight if you become exhausted first. You will probably lose because you no longer have the energy to continue fighting.

You need to learn how to manage your energy properly because, in BJJ, high stamina is crucial and gives you a superior level of control in a fight. Your goal is never to run out of fuel when you fight. By ensuring that you have excellent energy management skills, you will survive and outlast your opponent.

Following a healthy lifestyle will ensure you properly manage your energy at elevated levels continuously by sticking to a daily workout and training routine. Your goal is to be in the best shape and physical condition to avoid losing your energy quickly.

How to Maintain Maximum Energy during Your Fights?

Here are a few ways to ensure that your energy will be at an all-time high during your fights, boosting your chances of success.

Breathe Properly

In a BJJ fight, proper breathing focuses on pushing the air out via your nose or mouth rather than sucking the air in. Note that inhalation will come naturally on a completed exhalation, meaning that it's unnecessary to suck in the air again.

Another tip for proper breathing is to produce sounds every time you exhale. This way, you hear your exhalation occurring until you eventually become used to it.

The object of this exercise is that you monitor your breathing during the entire BJJ fight. Inhale through your nose and utilize your diaphragm for breathing rather than the upper portion of your lungs.

Develop Proper Mindset

When you've mastered proper breathing and control your breath effectively, you will notice that you easily control your mind. In a BJJ fight, your mindset also contributes to your energy levels. The goal is to stay calm even when dealing with pressure; otherwise, you will be at risk of losing your energy too fast.

One way to keep yourself calm during a fight is to focus on your breathing patterns, like exhaling more for a prolonged period. Also, learn to control your emotions, like excitement, fear, and anxiety. However, regardless of your BJJ level, you will still be at risk of feeling at least one of the above-mentioned emotions.

If you can't control them and use them to your best advantage, you will be at risk of losing your position, not thinking clearly about your next move, and falling into submission. Remember, these emotions come from your mind, so you have to develop the right mindset during your fights.

When in a BJJ match, being in the present moment ensures that your mind stays focused on your goal, and you can make wiser decisions. It will also help you control your emotions and prevent you from losing your energy, causing you to make even just a tiny slip that will compromise your accomplishments in a fight.

Chapter 11: Brazilian Jiu-Jitsu Versus Japanese Jiu-Jitsu

One common misconception of Jiu-Jitsu is that the Brazilian and Japanese variations are the same; it is easy to get confused. However, while there are similarities in history, origin, and techniques, there are also several differences.

This chapter illustrates what Brazilian Jiu-Jitsu and Japanese Jiu-Jitsu have in common – as well as their differences – so you can know the truths behind each misconception. Learning about the individual facts of each also helps you decide which the most suitable type of Jiu-Jitsu is for you.

What They Have in Common

The first similarity between Japanese and Brazilian Jiu-Jitsu is that both disciplines are closely related to Judo. If you are familiar with Kodokan Judo, you will realize that it is a modified variation of the traditional Japanese Jujutsu.

The birth of BJJ resulted from people's knowledge of Kodokan Judo, so it is safe to assume that Japanese Jiu-Jitsu and BJJ have an indirect relationship.

Apart from their indirect relationship as far as origin is concerned, there are similarities in some techniques, namely pins, leg locks, arm locks, chokeholds, and joint manipulations.

Another thing that makes the two so similar is that they are designed for participants regardless of their sizes and physical builds. Both are created to allow smaller participants to fight stronger and larger opponents. The skills and knowledge you can acquire from both martial arts are useful for self-defense, martial combat, and competitions.

The Differences

Brazilian Jiu-Jitsu and Japanese Jiu-Jitsu are also very different in many vital areas.

History

One significant area where the two greatly differ is in their history. Japanese Jiu-Jitsu came first and is even recognized as the oldest form of martial arts with roots that date back from 780AD to 1200AD. In the early 1300s, many used Japanese Jiu-Jitsu as a means to protect themselves from heavily armored and armed opponents on the battlefield.

During Japan's 17th century Edo period, Jujutsu and other forms of hand-to-hand combat became popular. It was also during this time that grappling arts were recognized together as Jujutsu.

In the later parts of the 1800s, Jigoro Kano, a jujutsu practitioner, made some changes in the art and started focusing more on submissions. He named this new art Kodokan Judo and started teaching it in Tokyo's Kodokan Institute. It led to the birth of modern Judo or Japanese Jiu-Jitsu.

BJJ's history is quite different. As discussed in an early chapter, the story of BJJ started after the creation of Judo, specifically when Judo experts started traveling around the world.

Some found themselves in Brazil introducing the art – one of whom was Mitsuyo Maeda, a Judo expert, master, and prizefighter. Maeda traveled around Brazil during the 1910s and 1920s, challenging many in other fighting arts. Eventually, Maeda and Carlos Gracie crossed paths, leading to the birth of Brazilian Jiu-Jitsu.

Rules

BJJ and Japanese Jiu-Jitsu have significant differences in their implemented rules. Japanese Jiu-Jitsu is more relaxed in that it does not hold the strong sports component BJJ has, evidenced by the competitions held worldwide.

As for the actual rules, BJJ competitions start with the two fighters in a standing position. They will attempt to take each other down or directly move to the guard, also called pulling guard. Upon bringing the fight to the ground, they will grapple to get their opponent to submit or get into a more dominant position and earn more points.

The fighter who is successful in making their opponent submit will instantly emerge as the winner. In the event of unsuccessful submission, the points earned by each will decide the winner of the match.

- 2 points for takedowns
- 3 points for a guard pass
- 2 points for knee-on-belly position
- 4 points for mount
- 4 points for back control
- 2 points for sweeps

Several Brazilian Jiu-Jitsu organizations hold competitions for this martial art every year, and each organization may have its own set of rules, but there is a high chance that most of these rules are similar.

Traditional Japanese Jiu-Jitsu does not come with a solid and strong sports competition environment like BJJ. However, you can still find modern offshoots for it, including the JJIF (Jiu-Jitsu International Federation). The competitions held by the JJIF come with three events – the duo, the fighting, and the Ne-Waza.

- **Duo** – Two practitioners have to do self-defense tactics randomly based on what the referee calls. The criteria for judgment would be control, reality, and power, among others.

- **Fighting** – This involves a 3-part competition where strikes are used in the initial stage of the fight. Once one fighter holds onto the other, it puts an end to the use of strikes. At this point, it is no longer permitted to use strikes, and the goal of the fighters is to take each other down.

Upon bringing the fight to the ground, the participants will use strangulations or joint locks to make the other submit. This event is scored on a points system, with the participants earning points based on their techniques throughout the match.

- **Ne-Waza** – The last one is very similar to the match or competition conducted in BJJ. It involves pitting two fighters against each other initially at a standing position, and the match does not allow using strikes.

The participants' goal is to bring their opponent down to the ground and forces them into submission using strangulation or joint lock. Participants will also earn points for dominant positions, throws, and takedowns.

Progression and Belts

BJJ and Japanese Jiu-Jitsu also have differences in the belt levels and how to progress in performance levels. BJJ utilizes a belt system comprised of eight belts.

- White for those still building a foundation
- Blue for technical proficiency
- Purple for game development, experimentation, and submissions
- Brown for conceptual thinking, strengthening of weaknesses, and setting traps
- Black for reflection and teaching and starting anew
- Red and black for seventh-degree black belt
- Red and white for eight-degree black belt
- Red for ninth and tenth-degree black belt

Every belt that falls below the black belt comes with four stripes demonstrating the skill level within a specific belt. The instructor has the authority to grant stripe and belt promotions. Also, note that every school has its own set of rules and policies on how to progress BJJ students.

Some schools may use a grading system for the stripes or belts granted to their students. The grades earned are based on the demonstrated sparring and techniques. Other schools depend entirely on their instructors for decisions regarding progression and promotion. So, you can earn a new belt based on your performance combined with technical knowledge, time or speed, and sparring proficiency.

Japanese Jiu-Jitsu also follows a different belt system, which depends on the school where you attend classes.

- White
- Yellow
- Orange
- Green
- Blue
- Purple
- Brown
- Black

Some schools provide a red belt to beginners before they get the white belt. On the other hand, other schools feature tips in between belts. Most Japanese Jiu-Jitsu school training requires students to participate in the formal grading system to progress to the following belt. The school will determine the specific techniques you must learn.

For instance, schools like the World Ju-jitsu Federation in Ireland require students to learn and display a specific number of tactics, a few Japanese terminologies, and a bit about anatomy.

Uniform

Both forms of martial arts require participants to wear the same uniform known as the Jiu-Jitsu Gi. However, these uniforms still differ in weight. The Gi used in BJJ is usually heavier than those used in karate, and the Japanese Jiu-Jitsu Gi is lighter than the Gi used in karate.

Aside from the clothing (Gi), BJJ students must also wear mouthguards for protection. Japanese Jiu-Jitsu students must wear groin guards to protect themselves from strikes that might inflict harm.

Important Technical and Technique Differences

The main focus of BJJ is grappling and also prioritizes ground fighting. BJJ participants will use strangles, joint locks, and chokes to make their opponents submit. Japanese Jiu-Jitsu focuses on joint manipulation, strikes, blocks, strangulations, chokes, and the throwing of opponents.

BJJ uses takedowns as a means of bringing their opponents down on the ground. Their focus is on establishing dominant positions to control their opponents and make them submit.

One of the most distinctive positions in Brazilian Jiu-Jitsu is the guard. It is an umbrella term covering various positions where participants lie on their buttocks or back with their legs defensively around or in front of their opponents. Many of the prospective techniques in BJJ are used for submitting opponents, moving into positions, and escaping positions.

Japanese Jiu-Jitsu participants gain knowledge by defending themselves from an attacker in various ways. Techniques are taught for submission or strikes to incapacitate attackers. Practicing these techniques will also involve sparring with a partner in different scenarios to block an attacker's initial punches and execute the joint lock. It is quite similar to BJJ as it also focuses on self-defense.

Brazilian and Japanese Jiu-Jitsu – The Pros and Cons

When deciding between Brazilian and Japanese Jiu-Jitsu, it is crucial to understand their pros and cons. You can better decide which of these two incredible martial arts is most suitable for you by deciphering their unique strengths and weaknesses.

BJJ Pros and Cons

One significant advantage of BJJ is that it is more fast-paced and physically demanding than Japanese Jiu-Jitsu. If you want rigorous workouts, BJJ is the right choice. What you learn from this martial art, including groundwork techniques, will make you more adept in competitions and matches.

Your improved skills in BJJ will allow several opportunities to attend competitions and high-level training as a partner and contested situational sparring. BJJ is also excellent for self-defense.

It teaches you how to use specific techniques whenever you're in a self-defense setting. Many fundamental techniques in BJJ, including escapes, back takes, and takedowns, are extremely useful for restraining your opponents or attackers.

However, BJJ also comes with its share of weaknesses. For one, it does not involve striking, which is highly useful in self-defense. BJJ also prioritizes teaching students about fighting on the ground, and in some instances, takedowns are ignored.

Japanese Jiu-Jitsu Pros and Cons

One advantage of Japanese Jiu-Jitsu is that it teaches you a plethora of skills and techniques to use for self-defense. In some instances, the training resembles real-life combat scenarios, but it does not train you to participate in competitions.

Also, your decision to learn Japanese Jiu-Jitsu will introduce you to valuable techniques you can use for fights and attackers, including strikes, throws, and groundwork.

It has its weakness, though. One is that it does not have the sparring training often included in BJJ classes. It also puts more emphasis on participants with low-level training, which is why their movements are calmer and more controlled than those of BJJ.

Aside from these, Japanese Jiu-Jitsu does not provide many opportunities for competitions, so it may not be suitable if you enjoy official matches and competitions.

Chapter 12: Daily BJJ Drills

Do you intend to become one of the greatest experts and masters in the world of Brazilian Jiu-Jitsu? Then just like the others who have already mastered this form of martial art, you must exert effort and spend endless hours practicing. It is not only the effort that brings you closer to your goal of mastering BJJ but your consistency and dedication.

The good news is that everyone can master this martial art, provided you are persistent and dedicated enough. One way to become adept in this field is to do BJJ drills regularly. With the BJJ drills you perform at home, you will internalize those unfamiliar motions.

Committing to a daily training regimen will be like sharpening your sword. Do this every day, and you will improve your body's flexibility, become less rigid, make it possible for your movements to flow smoothly, and execute your movements and techniques without any problem.

Your daily BJJ drills will also make you less prone to injury during a fight. This last chapter, a bonus chapter, educates you on the best daily BJJ drills you can use to begin your daily training and practice, regardless of where you are.

Use them to learn BJJ on your own or combine it with your actual classes to improve your expertise and knowledge further.

What Are BJJ Drills?

BJJ drills refer to a movement or a series of movements mimicking an actual match or sparring round scenario of BJJ. Some of the drills are doable alone, and others require you to do them with a partner. When doing BJJ drills, practice the specific technique to refine even the slightest component of your game. The drills are useful for improving general movement that you can apply in several positions during sparring.

Solo BJJ Drills

As mentioned earlier, solo BJJ drills are those you can do alone. These are a few examples.

Shrimp

A basic BJJ movement that you will learn during training or class is the shrimp. It should form part of your daily BJJ drills, as your mastery of this move can help you escape easily from a bad or unwanted position, such as under a mount or side control.

Plant one leg, then scoot your butt to one side. Use both hands on your other side, promoting ease in executing the movement and producing excellent results. Make this move as part of your warm-up exercises for as long as you want.

Technical Stand-up

This vital BJJ drill is perfect for beginners and is highly recommended to practice every day. Many consider it a safe and effective movement that allows you to get up after getting into a fallen position.

Start by sitting on the ground, bend your knees and place your feet flat on the floor. Tilt to one side, placing your leg and hip onto the floor. Your hand on the same side must also be palm flat on the floor, near your hip, and slightly back.

With the knee still bent, press on your other foot and put your weight on your free hand and your foot on the ground, pushing upward.

Reverse Shrimp

This is a reverse variation of the shrimp. It is a little harder to execute than the typical shrimp, but it has a lot of uses, such as setting yourself free from a north-south position, escaping from an armbar, and closing the gap or distance between you and your opponent.

Lie down on the floor with your legs straightened, and hold both your hands up. Choose a side to roll onto, then crunch down your shoulders based on your waist's direction and pivot using one shoulder.

Using your heels move your body so it faces in the direction of your feet. Extend both legs outward, and roll onto the other side. Repeat the steps.

Bridge to Shrimp

This is a move that you can also do alone, and it is useful if you are dealing with an opponent who has already mounted you. The bridge to shrimp will provide you with an effective means of escape.

The first thing to do is build a bridge by letting your butt go up in the air as you lie down on your back and execute the shrimp motion. It is a fantastic movement that is very effective if you want to improve your ability to escape from a bad or unwanted position.

Granby Roll

The Granby Roll is classified as a wrestling technique, but it is useful in Brazilian Jiu-Jitsu. It is a great technique for escaping inferior and bad positions and defending yourself from attacks. Be prepared to spend time practicing until you perfect it, and once you've mastered the technique, it will be relatively easy performing it.

Note that flexibility is not the ultimate key to performing a Granby roll. It is good mechanics. When you execute this move, avoid rolling on the back of your head or neck.

Begin this movement from your knees. Put one arm between your legs until you notice your shoulder touching the ground. It is important at this step to look away so you will not see your lowered shoulder. Raise yourself slightly to your toes, and this will bring both your knees off the mat.

Then crab walk in a specific direction. Your other shoulder will come close to the mat, and you should be looking at the ceiling between your legs.

Make sure that both your shoulders and feet are on the ground. Continue to crab walk until you go back to your knees.

Sprawls

Sprawls refer to defensive movements in BJJ combats, and you can perform them when countering your opponent's takedown strikes. Based on its name, sprawls require extending your body while aiming to pounce the opponent and dominate them.

Do this technique by first standing erect. Bend slightly and stretch both hands outward. Bring yourself down to the floor until your back is lying flat. Ensure that you let your palms support your entire body weight when doing so. Your legs also have to extend backward.

Keep your right leg straight and bend your left knee. Lift the middle part of your body quickly and squat walk to the right, pivoting your body on your palms. Do the same steps on the other side.

Non-Solo BJJ Drills

Non-solo BJJ drills are done if you do not have a training partner. It would be helpful to have a grappling dummy to perform these drills in the comfort of your home.

Leg Drag

This specific BJJ drill is a lot of fun and exciting at the same time, as it gives you an idea of how to improve your coordination. It is a fundamental move that will always form part of your training and practice in BJJ. Begin the leg drag drill by standing close to your partner or opponent.

Your opponent must lie on the ground with their feet on both sides of your hips. Grab one of their knees and shove it aside, specifically to one side of your body. This is necessary to pass the guard of your opponent. Repeat the steps.

Bridge Drill

This BJJ drill is also fun, though it could also be slightly harmful. Begin by lying by your opponent's side. Hold their legs and throw yourself so that you execute a front flip over the top of their body. Ensure that you land on your back and legs. Make sure you continue holding onto your opponent's legs while making the move. Repeat the steps but this time, do them on the other side.

Tornado Drill

This BJJ drill is similar to the leg drag, and the only difference is that this drill requires pulling the legs of your opponent to the side. Move to your side, then pass the guard of your opponent. Return to your initial position and repeat the same steps on the alternate side.

Conclusion

With discipline, commitment, hard work, and consistency, you will master Brazilian Jiu-Jitsu in no time. You must be prepared to go through all the training that teaches everything you need to know about this martial art.

BJJ is a lot of fun, especially for younger students, and provides many benefits. Rarely will you find a sport like Brazilian Jiu-Jitsu that offers tremendous mental and physical integration during every class and training session. It adds an element of fitness to your daily routine as you train to master this martial art.

Hopefully, this Brazilian Jiu-Jitsu book for beginners has helped jumpstart your journey toward mastering this art. Consult the information provided to improve your knowledge of BJJ and become a well-equipped participant.

Here's another book by Clint Sharp that you might like

CLINT SHARP

Kung-Fu

THE ULTIMATE
GUIDE
TO SHAOLIN
KUNG FU
ALONG WITH ITS
MOVEMENTS AND
TECHNIQUES

References

5 tips to improve your pressure jiu-jitsu style. (2020, February 24). Jiujitsu-News.Com. https://jiujitsu-news.com/5-tips-to-improve-your-pressure-Jiu-Jitsu-style/

40+ Brazilian Jiu Jitsu submissions you need to know. (2020, September 7). Bjjsuccess.Com. https://www.bjjsuccess.com/brazilian-Jiu-Jitsu-submissions/

Action reaction in Jiu-jitsu. (2020, January 29). Jiujitsu-News.Com. https://jiujitsu-news.com/action-reaction-in-Jiu-Jitsu/

Barra, G. (2014, July 31). 5 Tips on how to create pressure and be heavy on your opponent. - Gracie Barra. Graciebarra.Com. https://graciebarra.com/gb-news/tips-pressure-opponent/

Barra, G. (2021, January 25). Why Brazilian Jiu-Jitsu is the ultimate form of self-defense. Graciebarra.Com. https://graciebarra.com/chandler-az/why-brazilian-Jiu-Jitsu-is-good-for-self-defense/

Bjj, A. S. (n.d.). Learn BJJ Sequences - Combinations in Brazilian Jiu-Jitsu. Pureartbjj.Com. from https://www.pureartbjj.com/blog/bjj-sequences-combinations/

BJJ for self defence: A complete review by an ex cop. (2020). https://theselfdefenceexpert.com/bjj-for-self-defence/

BJJEE. (2020a, February 20). How to successfully use action-reaction principles when grappling. Bjjee.Com. https://www.bjjee.com/articles/successfully-use-action-reaction-principles-grappling/

BJJEE. (2020b, April 14). Marcelo Garcia on how to use combinations to finish opponents. Bjjee.Com. https://www.bjjee.com/articles/marcelo-garcia-on-how-to-use-combinations-to-finish-opponents/

bjjmindset. (2013, June 7). Action and Reaction. Wordpress.Com. https://bjjmindset.wordpress.com/2013/06/07/action-and-reaction/

BjjTribes. (2020, September 20). How many guards are there in BJJ? The Ultimate list of all of the guard positions in Brazilian Jiu Jitsu. Bjjtribes.Com. https://bjjtribes.com/list-of-all-of-the-guard-positions-in-brazilian-Jiu-Jitsu/

Brazilian Jiu Jitsu – everything about the gentle art. (2019, October 3). Bjj-World.Com. https://bjj-world.com/brazilian-Jiu-Jitsu/

Brazilian jiu jitsu what is it. (2020, April 29). Jiujitsu-News.Com. https://jiujitsu-news.com/brazilian-Jiu-Jitsu-what-is-it/

Brazilian Jiu-jitsu style. (2020, January 29). Jiujitsu-News.Com. https://jiujitsu-news.com/brazilian-Jiu-Jitsu-style/

Bryers, M. (2018, December 13). Top 3 Takedowns For Brazilian Jiu Jitsu. Jiujitsuct.Com. https://www.jiujitsuct.com/3-takedowns-bjj

de Los Reyes, J. (2016, June 15). The Strengths and Weaknesses of Each Martial Art for self-defense. Kombatarts.Com. https://kombatarts.com/strengths-weaknesses-martial-art-self-defense/

Evolve, M. M. A. (2018a, January 29). The first 3 submissions you should master in Brazilian Jiu-Jitsu. Evolve-Mma.Com. https://evolve-mma.com/blog/the-first-3-submissions-you-should-master-in-brazilian-Jiu-Jitsu/

Evolve, M. M. A. (2018b, March 31). 5 basic BJJ movements beginners need to perfect. Evolve-Mma.Com. https://evolve-mma.com/blog/5-basic-bjj-movements-beginners-need-to-perfect/

Evolve, M. M. A. (2019, January 6). The 3 best BJJ takedowns for beginners. Evolve-Mma.Com. https://evolve-mma.com/blog/the-3-best-bjj-takedowns-for-beginners/

Fanatics Authors. (n.d.). Five Essential BJJ Takedowns! Bjjfanatics.Com. from https://bjjfanatics.com/blogs/news/five-essential-bjj-takedowns

Four Esoteric Principles of Martial Arts Skill Development. (2019, December 3). Sonnybrown.Net. https://www.sonnybrown.net/principles-martial-arts-skill-development/

Freeman, D. (2021a, May 14). Brazilian Jiu-Jitsu vs Japanese Jiu-Jitsu: The difference you should know. Bjjgireviews.Com. https://bjjgireviews.com/brazilian-Jiu-Jitsu-vs-japanese-Jiu-Jitsu/

Freeman, D. (2021b, May 26). 10 tips to get started in Brazilian Jiu-jitsu (2021). Bjjgireviews.Com. https://bjjgireviews.com/get-started-in-bjj/

Freeman, D. (2021c, June 3). best BJJ Solo Drills you can do at home by yourself (EVERYDAY). Bjjgireviews.Com. https://bjjgireviews.com/bjj-solo-drills

guy. (2019, September 20). 8 Mistakes Typically made by Brazilian Jiu-Jitsu Beginners. Bjjnc.Com. https://www.bjjnc.com/8-mistakes-typically-made-by-brazilian-Jiu-Jitsu-beginners/

How all Brazilian Jiu-Jitsu Submission Holds work. (2020, September 2). Bjj-World.Com. https://bjj-world.com/brazilian-Jiu-Jitsu-submission-holds/

Intermediate bjj: Building submission combinations. (2016, March 31). Jiujitsutimes.Com. https://jiujitsutimes.com/intermediate-bjj-building-submission-combinations/

Jiu Jitsu, L. (2020, April 1). 10 best BJJ drills you can do home alone. Jiujitsulegacy.Com. https://jiujitsulegacy.com/health/strength-conditioning/10-best-bjj-drills-you-can-do-home-alone/

Jiu-jitsu fight energy Management. (2020, January 29). Jiujitsu-News.Com. https://jiujitsu-news.com/Jiu-Jitsu-fight-energy-management/

Kesting, S. (2016, June 18). 37 powerful BJJ submissions for grapplers. Grapplearts.Com. https://www.grapplearts.com/37-powerful-bjj-submissions-for-grapplers/

Kesting, S. (2018, January 16). Japanese Jiujitsu vs BJJ. Grapplearts.Com. https://www.grapplearts.com/japanese-jiujitsu-vs-bjj/

Kesting, S. (2021, March 1). Top 10 throws and takedowns for BJJ. Grapplearts.Com. https://www.grapplearts.com/top-10-throws-and-takedowns-for-bjj/

leticiamedeiros. (2018, November 26). Takedowns for Jiu-jitsu - Gracie Barra. Graciebarra.Com. https://graciebarra.com/gb-learning/takedowns-for-Jiu-Jitsu/

Marlin, S. (2018, December 14). The Difference Between jiu jitsu vs bjj. Martialboss.Com. https://martialboss.com/Jiu-Jitsu-vs-bjj

Martial arts grappling techniques (beginner & advanced). (2018, September 7). Blackbeltwiki.Com. https://blackbeltwiki.com/grappling

Open guard vs closed guard BJJ explained. (2021, January 27). Jiujitsu-News.Com. https://jiujitsu-news.com/open-guard-vs-closed-guard/

Ruiz, B. (2020, May 11). 23 effective bjj takedowns. Mma-Today.Com. https://www.mma-today.com/bjj-takedowns-judo-throws/

Scandinavia, B. J. J. (2016, October 13). All guards in Brazilian Jiu Jitsu (with videos) - BJJ Scandinavia. Bjjscandinavia.Com. http://www.bjjscandinavia.com/2016/10/13/all-guards-in-brazilian-Jiu-Jitsu-with-videos/

Skoczylas, N. (2020a, October 19). Japanese Jiu-jitsu vs. Brazilian Jiu-jitsu. Projectbjj.Com. https://projectbjj.com/japanese-Jiu-Jitsu-vs-brazilian-Jiu-Jitsu/

Skoczylas, N. (2020b, October 28). What are the fundamentals in Brazilian Jiu-Jitsu? Projectbjj.Com. https://projectbjj.com/what-are-the-fundamentals-in-brazilian-Jiu-Jitsu/

Smith, A. (2017, November 11). Combinations in BJJ. HowTheyPlay. https://howtheyplay.com/individual-sports/Combinations-in-BJJ

Spot, B. (2017, November 20). 6 common BJJ mistakes you should avoid. Bjj-Spot.Com. https://www.bjj-spot.com/common-bjj-mistakes/

Spot, B. (2018a, April 29). Basic BJJ Drills you should do every day. Bjj-Spot.Com. https://www.bjj-spot.com/basic-bjj-drills/

Spot, B. (2018b, September 27). Guard retention – important moves and principles. Bjj-Spot.Com. https://www.bjj-spot.com/guard-retention/

The 17 time-tested benefits of Brazilian Jiu Jitsu. (2020, February 11). Bjjsuccess.Com. https://www.bjjsuccess.com/benefits-of-brazilian-Jiu-Jitsu/

The Benefits of Taking a Grappling Class. (n.d.). Nymaa.Com. from https://www.nymaa.com/martial-arts-blog/The-Benefits-of-Taking-a-Grappling-Class_AE92.html

The best modern BJJ stretching routine for improved grappling. (2020, April 27). Bjjsuccess.Com. https://www.bjjsuccess.com/stretching-for-bjj/

The fundamental BJJ submissions. (2020, November 4). Youjiujitsu.Com. https://youjiujitsu.com/the-fundamental-bjj-submissions/

The pressure game in Jiu-Jitsu. (2015, March 23). Jiujitsutimes.Com. https://jiujitsutimes.com/the-pressure-game-in-Jiu-Jitsu/

The top 4 bjj self defence techniques you should know. (2016, March 10). Jiujitsutimes.Com. https://jiujitsutimes.com/the-top-4-bjj-self-defence-techniques-you-should-know/

The true history of Brazilian Jiu jitsu. (2020, April 9). Bjjsuccess.Com. https://www.bjjsuccess.com/history-of-brazilian-Jiu-Jitsu/

The ULTIMATE analysis of "PRESSURE." (2016, June 19). Jiujitsutimes.Com. https://jiujitsutimes.com/ultimate-analysis-pressure/

The ultimate Brazilian Jiu jitsu guide for beginners. (2020, January 4). Middleeasy.Com. https://middleeasy.com/guides/Jiu-Jitsu-guide/

(N.d.-a). Findyourgi.Com. Retrieved from https://findyourgi.com/what-is-bjj/

(N.d.-b). Letsrollbjj.Com. Retrieved from https://www.letsrollbjj.com/bjj-white-belt-tips/

5 qualities to look for in a Brazilian Jiu-Jitsu instructor. (2016, February 27). Jiujitsutimes.Com. https://jiujitsutimes.com/5-qualities-to-look-for-in-a-brazilian-jiu-jitsu-instructor/

Barra, G. (2015, July 4). The "secret" to getting better at BJJ - Gracie Barra. Graciebarra.Com. https://graciebarra.com/gb-news/the-secret-bjj/

Battle Arts Academy. (2019, December 28). How to get better at Brazilian Jiu-Jitsu: The top tips for beginners. Battleartsacademy.Ca. https://www.battleartsacademy.ca/post/how-to-get-better-at-brazilian-jiu-jitsu-the-top-tips-for-beginners

Park, J. (2014, June 13). 57 Training Tips for Brazilian Jiu Jitsu White Belts. Crazy88mma.Com. https://www.crazy88mma.com/57-training-tips-for-brazilian-jiu-jitsu-white-belts/

Printed in the USA
CPSIA information can be obtained
at www.ICGtesting.com
LVHW011054260124
770060LV00004B/30